FIX-IT and FORGET-IT®
BEST SLOW COOKER
CHICKEN RECIPES

FIX-IT and FORGET-IT®
BEST SLOW COOKER
CHICKEN RECIPES
QUICK AND EASY DINNERS, CASSEROLES, SOUPS, STEWS, AND MORE!

HOPE COMERFORD

Good Books

New York, New York

Library of Congress Cataloging-in-Publication Data is available on file.

Cover design by Abigail Gehring
Cover photo by Meredith Special Interest Media

Print ISBN: 978-1-68099-455-1
Ebook ISBN: 978-1-68099-458-2

Printed in China

Table of Contents

Welcome to Fix-It and Forget-It Slow Cooker Chicken Recipes

Love chicken? So do we! That's why we've put together an entire book of chicken recipes for your enjoyment. To make it even easier for you, we've compiled many recipes that are 5 Ingredients or Fewer and 10 Ingredients or Fewer. Our hope is it helps you make the most of your time. We've also included some other chicken recipes that include 11 Ingredients or More for when you have more time, chicken soup recipes, wing recipes, and even recipes that use pre-cooked chicken (for when you have leftover chicken to use up). You're going to love not having to search through multiple cookbooks to find the perfect chicken recipe!

Choosing a Slow Cooker

Not all slow cookers are created equal . . . or work equally as well for everyone!

Those of us who use slow cookers frequently know we have our own preferences when it comes to which slow cooker we choose to use. For instance, I love my programmable slow cooker, but there are many programmable slow cookers I've tried that I've strongly disliked. Why? Because some go by increments of 15 or 30 minutes and some go by 4, 6, 8, or 10 hours. I dislike those restrictions, but I have family and friends who don't mind them at all! I am also pretty brand loyal when it comes to my manual slow cookers because I've had great success with those and have had unsuccessful moments with slow cookers of other brands. So, which slow cooker(s) is/are best for your household?

It really depends on how many people you're feeding and if you're gone for long periods of time. Here are my recommendations:

For 2–3 person household	3–5 quart slow cooker
For 4–5 person household	5–6 quart slow cooker
For a 6+ person household	6½–7 quart slow cooker

Large slow cooker advantages/disadvantages:

Advantages:
- You can fit a loaf pan or a baking dish into a 6- or 7–quart, depending on the shape of your cooker. That allows you to make bread or cakes, or even smaller quantities of main dishes. (Take your favorite baking dish and loaf pan along when you shop for a cooker to make sure they'll fit inside.)
- You can feed large groups of people, or make larger quantities of food, allowing for leftovers, or meals, to freeze.

Disadvantages:
- They take up more storage room.
- They don't fit as neatly into a dishwasher.
- If your crock isn't ⅔–¾ full, you may burn your food.

Small slow cooker advantages/disadvantages:

Advantages:
- They're great for lots of appetizers, for serving hot drinks, for baking cakes straight in the crock, and for dorm rooms or apartments.
- Great option for making recipes of smaller quantities.

Disadvantages:
- Food in smaller quantities tends to cook more quickly than larger amounts. So keep an eye on it.
- Chances are, you won't have many leftovers. So, if you like to have leftovers, a smaller slow cooker may not be a good option for you.

My recommendation:

Have at least two slow cookers; one around 3 to 4 quarts and one 6 quarts or larger. A third would be a huge bonus (and a great advantage to your cooking repertoire!). The advantage of having at least a couple is you can make a larger variety of recipes. Also, you can make at least two or three dishes at once for a whole meal.

Manual vs. Programmable

If you are gone for only six to eight hours a day, a manual slow cooker might be just fine for you. If you are gone for more than eight hours during the day, I would highly recommend purchasing a programmable slow cooker that will switch to warm when the cook time you set is up. It will allow you to cook a wider variety of recipes.

The two I use most frequently are my 4–quart manual slow cooker and my 6½–quart programmable slow cooker. I like that I can make smaller portions in my 4–quart slow cooker on days I don't need or want leftovers, but I also love how my 6½–quart slow cooker can accommodate whole chickens, turkey breasts, hams, or big batches of soups. I use them both often.

Get to know your slow cooker . . .

Plan a little time to get acquainted with your slow cooker. Each slow cooker has its own personality—just like your oven (and your car). Plus, many new slow cookers cook hotter and faster than earlier models. I think that with all of the concern for food safety, the slow cooker manufacturers have amped up their settings so that "High," "Low," and "Warm" are all higher temperatures than in the older models. That means they cook hotter—and therefore, faster—than the first slow cookers. The beauty of these little machines is that they're supposed to cook low and slow. We count on that when we flip the switch in the morning before we leave the house for ten hours or so. So, because none of us knows what kind of temperament our slow cooker has until we try it out, nor how hot it cooks—don't assume anything. Save yourself a disappointment and make the first recipe in your new slow cooker on a day when you're at home. Cook it for the shortest amount of time the recipe calls for. Then, check the food to see if it's done. Or if you start smelling food that seems to be finished, turn off the cooker and rescue your food.

Also, all slow cookers seem to have a "hot spot," which is of great importance to know, especially when baking with your slow cooker. This spot may tend to burn food in that area if you're not careful. If you're baking directly in your slow cooker, I recommend covering the "hot spot" with some foil.

Take notes . . .

Don't be afraid to make notes in your cookbook. It's yours! Chances are, it will eventually get passed down to someone in your family and they will love and appreciate all of your musings. Take note of which slow cooker you used and exactly how long it took to cook the recipe. The next time you make it, you won't need to try to remember. Apply what you learned to the next recipes you make in your cooker. If another recipe says it needs to cook 7–9 hours, and you've discovered your slow cooker cooks on the faster side, cook that recipe for 6–6½ hours and then check it. You can always cook a recipe longer—but you can't reverse things if it's overdone.

Get creative . . .

If you know your morning is going to be hectic, prepare everything the night before, take it out so the crock warms up to room temperature when you first get up in the morning, then plug it in and turn it on as you're leaving the house.

   If you want to make something that has a short cook time and you're going to be gone longer than that, cook it the night before and refrigerate it for the next day. Warm it up when you get home. Or, cook those recipes on the weekend when you know you'll be home and eat them later in the week.

Slow Cooking Tips and Tricks and Other Things You May Not Know

- Slow cookers tend to work best when they're ⅔ to ¾ of the way full. You may need to increase the cooking time if you've exceeded that amount, or reduce it if you've put in less than that. If you're going to exceed that limit, it would be best to reduce the recipe, or split it between two slow cookers. (Remember how I suggested owning at least two or three slow cookers?)
- Keep your veggies on the bottom. That puts them in more direct contact with the heat. The fuller your slow cooker, the longer it will take its contents to cook. Also, the more densely packed the cooker's contents are, the longer they will take to cook. And finally, the larger the chunks of meat or vegetables, the more time they will need to cook.
- Keep the lid on! Every time you take a peek, you lose 20 minutes of cooking time. Please take this into consideration each time you lift the lid! I know, some of you can't help yourself and are going to lift anyway. Just don't forget to tack on 20 minutes to your cook time for each time you peeked!
- Sometimes it's beneficial to remove the lid. If you'd like your dish to thicken a bit, take the lid off during the last half hour to hour of cooking time.
- If you have a big slow cooker (7- to 8-quart), you can cook a small batch in it by putting the recipe ingredients into an oven-safe baking dish or baking pan and then placing that into the cooker's crock. First, put a trivet or some metal jar rings on the bottom of the crock, and then set your dish or pan on top of them. Or a loaf pan may "hook onto" the top ridges of the crock belonging to a large oval cooker and hang there straight and securely, "baking" a cake or quick bread. Cover the cooker and flip it on.

- The outside of your slow cooker will be hot! Please remember to keep it out of reach of children and keep that in mind for yourself as well!
- Get yourself a quick–read meat thermometer and use it! This helps remove the question of whether or not your meat is fully cooked, and helps prevent you from overcooking your meat as well.

Internal Cooking Temperatures:
  - Beef—125–130°F (rare); 140–145°F (medium); 160°F (well–done)
  - Pork—140–145°F (rare); 145–150°F (medium); 160°F (well–done)
  - Turkey and Chicken—165°F
  - Frozen meat: The basic rule of thumb is, don't put frozen meat into the slow cooker. The meat does not reach the proper internal temperature in time. This especially applies to thick cuts of meat! Proceed with caution!

- Add fresh herbs 10 minutes before the end of the cooking time to maximize their flavor.
- If your recipe calls for cooked pasta, add it 10 minutes before the end of the cooking time if the cooker is on High; 30 minutes before the end of the cooking time if it's on Low. Then the pasta won't get mushy.
- If your recipe calls for sour cream or cream, stir it in 5 minutes before the end of the cooking time. You want it to heat but not boil or simmer.

Approximate Slow Cooker Temperatures (Remember, each slow cooker is different):
  - High—212°F–300°F
  - Low—170°F–200°F
  - Simmer—185°F
  - Warm—165°F

Cooked beans freeze well. Store them in freezer bags (squeeze the air out first) or freezer boxes. Cooked and dried bean measurements:
  - 16-oz. can, drained = about 1¾ cups beans
  - 19-oz. can, drained = about 2 cups beans
  - 1 lb. dried beans (about 2½ cups) = 5 cups cooked beans

5 Ingredients or Fewer

Bone-In Lemon Honey Chicken

Carolyn W. Carmichael, Berkeley Heights, NJ

Makes 4–6 servings
Prep. Time: 5 minutes ⚜ Cooking Time: 8 hours ⚜ Ideal slow-cooker size: 4-qt.

1 lemon
1 whole roasting chicken, rinsed
½ cup orange juice
½ cup honey

1. Pierce lemon with fork. Place in chicken cavity. Place chicken in slow cooker.

2. Combine orange juice and honey. Pour over chicken.

3. Cover. Cook on Low 8 hours. Remove lemon and squeeze over chicken.

4. Carve chicken and serve.

Chicken Marengo

Marcia Parker, Lansdale, PA

Makes 4–5 servings
Prep Time: 5–10 minutes ⚬ *Cooking Time: 6–7 hours* ⚬ *Ideal slow-cooker size: 6-qt.*

2½–3-lb. frying chicken,
cut-up and skinned

2 envelopes dry spaghetti sauce mix

½ cup dry white wine

2 fresh tomatoes, quartered

¼ lb. fresh mushrooms

1. Place chicken pieces in the bottom of your slow cooker.

2. In a small bowl, combine the dry spaghetti sauce mix with the wine. Pour it over the chicken.

3. Cover and cook on Low 5½–6½ hours.

4. Turn temperature to High. Then add tomatoes and mushrooms.

5. Cover and cook on High 30–40 minutes or until the vegetables are hot.

6. Serve with cooked noodles or your favorite other pasta.

Poached Chicken

Mary E. Wheatley, Mashpee, MA

Makes 6 servings
Prep Time: 15 minutes ॐ *Cooking Time: 7–8 hours* ॐ *Ideal slow-cooker size: 4½-qt.*

1 whole broiler-fryer chicken, about 3 lb.

1 celery rib, cut into chunks

1 carrot, sliced

1 medium-sized onion, sliced

1 cup chicken broth, seasoned, or water, or dry white wine

1. Wash chicken. Pat dry with paper towels and place in slow cooker.

2. Place celery, carrot, and onion around chicken. Pour broth over all.

3. Cover and cook on Low 7–8 hours, or until chicken is tender.

4. Remove chicken from pot and place on platter. When cool enough to handle, debone.

5. Strain broth into a container and chill.

6. Place chunks of meat in fridge or freezer until ready to use in salads or main dishes.

Herby Chicken

Joyce Bowman, Lady Lake, FL

Makes 4–6 servings
Prep Time: 10 minutes ⚬ *Cooking Time: 5–7 hours* ⚬ *Ideal slow-cooker size: 5-qt.*

2½–3½-lb. whole roaster chicken

1 lemon, cut into wedges

1 bay leaf

2–4 sprigs fresh thyme,
or ¾ tsp. dried thyme

Salt and pepper to taste

1. Remove giblets from chicken.

2. Put lemon wedges and bay leaf in cavity.

3. Place whole chicken in slow cooker.

4. Scatter sprigs of thyme over the chicken. Sprinkle with salt and pepper.

5. Cover and cook on Low 5–7 hours, or until chicken is tender.

6. Serve hot with pasta or rice, or debone and freeze for your favorite casseroles or salads.

Roast Chicken

Betty Drescher, Quakertown, PA

Makes 6 servings
Prep Time: 30 minutes ⚬ *Cooking Time: 9–11 hours* ⚬ *Ideal slow-cooker size: 4- to 5-qt.*

3–4-lb. roasting chicken, or hen
1½ tsp. salt
¼ tsp. pepper
1 tsp. parsley flakes, *divided*
1 Tbsp. butter
½–1 cup water

1. Thoroughly wash chicken and pat dry.

2. Sprinkle cavity with salt, pepper, and ½ tsp. parsley flakes. Place in slow cooker, breast side up.

3. Dot with butter or brush with melted butter.

4. Sprinkle with remaining parsley flakes. Add water around the chicken.

5. Cover and cook on High 1 hour. Turn to Low and cook 8–10 hours.

TIPS

1. Sprinkle with basil or tarragon in Step 4, if you wish.

2. To make it a more complete meal, put carrots, onions, and celery in the bottom of the slow cooker.

Oregano Chicken

Tina Goss, Duenweg, MO

Makes 6 servings
Prep Time: 5 minutes ⚜ *Cooking Time: 4–6 hours* ⚜ *Ideal slow-cooker size: 4- to 5-qt.*

3½–4 lb. chicken, cut-up

Half a stick (¼ cup) butter, or margarine, melted

1 envelope dry Italian salad dressing mix

2 Tbsp. lemon juice

1–2 Tbsp. dried oregano

1. Place chicken in bottom of slow cooker. Mix butter, dressing mix, and lemon juice together and pour over top.

2. Cover and cook on High for 4–6 hours, or until chicken is tender but not dry.

3. Baste occasionally with sauce mixture and sprinkle with oregano 1 hour or just before serving.

Tender Barbecued Chicken

Mary Lynn Miller, Reinholds, PA

Makes 4–6 servings
Prep Time: 10–15 minutes ⚜ *Cooking Time: 8–10 hours* ⚜ *Ideal slow-cooker size: 5-qt.*

3–4-lb. broiler/fryer chicken, cut up
1 medium-sized onion, thinly sliced
1 medium-sized lemon, thinly sliced
18-oz. bottle barbecue sauce
¾ cup cola

1. Place chicken in slow cooker. Top with onion and lemon slices.

2. Combine barbecue sauce and cola. Pour over all.

3. Cover and cook on Low 8–10 hours, or until chicken is tender but not dry.

Honey Baked Chicken

Mary Kennell, Roanoke, IL

Makes 4 servings
Prep Time: 15 minutes   Cooking Time: 3–6 hours   Ideal slow-cooker size: 5-qt.

4 skinless, bone-in chicken breast halves

2 Tbsp. butter, melted

2 Tbsp. honey

2 tsp. prepared mustard

2 tsp. curry powder

Salt and pepper, optional

1. Spray slow cooker with non-stick cooking spray and add chicken.

2. Mix butter, honey, mustard, and curry powder together in a small bowl. Pour sauce over chicken.

3. Cover and cook on High 3 hours, or on Low 5–6 hours.

Variations:

1. Use chicken thighs instead of breasts. Drop the curry powder if you wish.

—Cathy Boshart, Lebanon, PA

2. Use a small fryer chicken, quartered, instead of breasts or thighs.

—Frances Kruba, Dundalk, MD

3. Instead of curry powder, use ½ tsp. paprika.

—Jena Hammond, Traverse City, MI

Orange Garlic Chicken

Susan Kasting, Jenks, OK

Makes 6 servings

Prep Time: 15 minutes ❧ *Cooking Time: 2½–6 hours* ❧ *Ideal slow-cooker size: 4-qt.*

6 skinless, bone-in chicken breast halves

1½ tsp. dry thyme

6 cloves garlic, minced

1 cup orange juice concentrate

2 Tbsp. balsamic vinegar

1. Rub thyme and garlic over chicken. (Reserve any leftover thyme and garlic.) Place chicken in slow cooker.

2. Mix orange juice concentrate and vinegar together in a small bowl. Stir in reserved thyme and garlic. Spoon over chicken.

3. Cover and cook on Low 5–6 hours, or on High 2½–3 hours, or until chicken is tender but not dry.

TIP
Remove chicken from slow cooker and keep warm on a platter. Skim fat from sauce. Bring remaining sauce to boil in a saucepan to reduce. Serve sauce over chicken and cooked rice.

Chicken Cacciatore with Green Peppers

Donna Lantgen, Chadron, NE

Makes 6 servings
Prep Time: 10 minutes ⚬ Cooking Time: 6 hours ⚬ Ideal slow-cooker size: 5-qt.

1 green pepper, chopped
1 onion, chopped
1 Tbsp. dry Italian seasoning
15½-oz. can diced tomatoes
6 boneless, skinless chicken breast halves, divided

1. In a small bowl, mix together green pepper, onion, Italian seasoning, and tomatoes. Place ⅓ in bottom of slow cooker.

2. Layer 3 chicken breasts over top. Spoon in ⅓ of tomato sauce.

3. Layer in 3 remaining chicken breasts. Top with remaining tomato mixture.

4. Cover and cook on Low 6 hours, or until chicken is done, but not dry.

Variation:

Top with grated mozzarella or Parmesan cheese when serving.

Chicken Parmigiana

Lois Ostrander, Lebanon, PA

Makes 6 servings
Prep Time: 20 minutes ♣ Cooking Time: 6–8 hours ♣ Ideal slow-cooker size: 3½-qt.

I egg

I cup dry bread crumbs

6 bone-in chicken breast halves, *divided*

10½-oz. jar pizza sauce, *divided*

6 slices mozzarella cheese,
or ½ cup grated Parmesan cheese

1. Beat egg in a shallow, oblong bowl. Place bread crumbs in another shallow, oblong bowl. Dip chicken halves into egg, and then into the crumbs, using a spoon to coat the meat on all sides with crumbs.

2. Saute chicken in a large non-stick skillet sprayed with non-stick cooking spray.

3. Arrange 1 layer of browned chicken in slow cooker. Pour half the pizza sauce over top. Add a second layer of chicken. Pour remaining pizza sauce over top.

4. Cover and cook on Low 5¾–7¾ hours, or until chicken is tender but not dry.

5. Add mozzarella cheese or Parmesan cheese on top. Cover and cook 15 more minutes.

TIPS

1. You can remove the chicken from the slow cooker after Step 4 and place the breasts on a microwave-proof serving platter. Put a slice of mozzarella on each chicken piece and then sprinkle each with Parmesan. Cook in microwave on High for 1 minute to melt cheese.

2. Serve any extra sauce over pasta.

Come–Back–for–More Barbecued Chicken

Leesa DeMartyn, Enola, PA

Makes 6–8 servings

Prep Time: 10 minutes ⚘ *Cooking Time: 6–8 hours* ⚘ *Ideal slow-cooker size: 5-qt.*

6–8 chicken breast halves

I cup ketchup

⅓ cup Worcestershire sauce

½ cup brown sugar

I tsp. chili powder

½ cup water

1. Place chicken in slow cooker.

2. Whisk remaining ingredients in a large bowl. Pour sauce mixture over chicken.

3. Cover and cook on Low for 6–8 hours, or until chicken is tender but not overcooked.

TIP

If the sauce begins to dry out as the dish cooks, stir in another ½ cup water.

Tangy Chicken Legs

Frances L. Kruba, Dundalk, MD

Makes 4–6 servings
Prep Time: 10–15 minutes ❧ Cooking Time: 4–5 hours ❧ Ideal slow-cooker size: 5- to 6-qt. (oblong is best)

8 chicken drumsticks
⅓ cup soy sauce
⅔ cup packed brown sugar
Scant ⅛ tsp. ground ginger
¼ cup water

1. Place chicken in slow cooker.

2. Combine remaining ingredients in a bowl and spoon over chicken.

3. Cover and cook on Low 4–5 hours, or until chicken is tender but not dry.

Raspberried Chicken Drumsticks

Pat Bechtel, Dillsburg, PA

Makes 3 servings

Prep Time: 10 minutes ⚶ *Cooking Time: 5¼–6¼ hours* ⚶ *Ideal slow-cooker size: 3½-qt.*

3 Tbsp. soy sauce

⅓ cup red raspberry fruit spread or jam

5 chicken drumsticks or chicken thighs

2 Tbsp. cornstarch

2 Tbsp. cold water

1. Mix soy sauce and raspberry spread or jam together in a small bowl until well blended.

2. Brush chicken with the sauce and place in slow cooker. Spoon remainder of the sauce over top.

3. Cook on Low 5–6 hours, or until chicken is tender but not dry.

4. Mix together cornstarch and cold water in a small bowl until smooth. Then remove chicken to a serving platter and keep warm. Turn slow cooker to High and stir in cornstarch and water to thicken. When thickened and bubbly, after about 10–15 minutes, spoon sauce over chicken before serving.

Cranberry Chicken Barbecue

Gladys M. High, Ephrata, PA

Makes 6–8 servings
Prep Time: 10 minutes ⚜ *Cooking Time: 4–8 hours* ⚜ *Ideal slow-cooker size: 4- to 5-qt.*

4 lb. chicken pieces, *divided*

½ tsp. salt

¼ tsp. pepper

16-oz. can whole–berry cranberry sauce

1 cup barbecue sauce

Optional ingredients:

½ cup diced celery

½ cup diced carrots

½ cup diced onion

1. Place ⅓ of the chicken pieces in the slow cooker.

2. Combine all sauce ingredients in a mixing bowl. Spoon ⅓ of the sauce over the chicken in the cooker.

3. Repeat Steps 1 and 2 twice.

4. Cover and bake on High 4 hours, or on Low 6–8 hours, or until chicken is tender but not dry.

Chicken with Vegetables

Janie Steele, Moore, OK

Makes 4 servings
Prep Time: 10–15 minutes ☙ Cooking Time: 6–8 hours ☙ Ideal slow-cooker size: 6-qt.

4 bone-in chicken breast halves

1 small head of cabbage, quartered

1-lb. pkg. baby carrots

2 (14½-oz.) cans Mexican-flavored stewed tomatoes

1. Place all ingredients in slow cooker in order listed.

2. Cover and cook on Low 6–8 hours, or until chicken and vegetables are tender.

Lemon Pepper Chicken and Veggies

Nadine Martinitz, Salina, KS

Makes 4 servings

Prep Time: 20 minutes & Cooking Time: 4–10 hours & Ideal slow-cooker size: 4-qt.

4 carrots, sliced ½" thick

4 potatoes, cut in 1" chunks

2 cloves garlic, peeled and minced, *optional*

4 whole chicken legs and thighs, skin removed

2 tsp. lemon pepper seasoning

¼ –½ tsp. poultry seasoning, *optional*

14½-oz. can chicken broth

1. Layer vegetables and chicken in slow cooker.

2. Sprinkle with lemon pepper seasoning and poultry seasoning if you wish. Pour broth over all.

3. Cover and cook on Low 8–10 hours or on High 4–5 hours.

Variations:

1. Use a 10 ¾-oz. can cream of chicken or mushroom soup instead of chicken broth.

—Sarah Herr, Goshen, IN

2. Add 2 cups frozen green beans to the bottom layer (Step 1) in the cooker.

— Earnest Zimmerman, Mechanicsburg, PA

Spanish Chicken

Natalia Showalter, Mt. Solon, VA

Makes 4–6 servings
Prep Time: 15–20 minutes ❧ *Cooking Time: 5–6 hours* ❧ *Ideal slow-cooker size: 3- to 6-qt.*

8 chicken thighs, skinned

½–1 cup red wine vinegar, according to your taste preference

⅔ cup tamari, or low-sodium soy sauce

1 tsp. garlic powder

4 6" cinnamon sticks

1. Brown chicken slightly in non-stick skillet, if you wish, and then transfer to greased slow cooker.

2. Mix wine vinegar, tamari sauce, and garlic powder together in a bowl. Pour over chicken.

3. Break cinnamon sticks into several pieces and distribute among chicken thighs.

4. Cover and cook on Low 5–6 hours, or until chicken is tender but not dry.

Thai Chicken

Joanne Good, Wheaton, IL

Makes 6 servings
Prep Time: 5 minutes & Cooking Time: 8–9 hours & Ideal slow-cooker size: 4-qt.

6 skinless chicken thighs

¾ cup salsa, your choice of mild, medium, or hot

¼ cup chunky peanut butter

1 Tbsp. low-sodium soy sauce

2 Tbsp. lime juice

Optional ingredients:

1 tsp. gingerroot, grated

2 Tbsp. cilantro, chopped

1 Tbsp. dry-roasted peanuts, chopped

1. Put chicken in slow cooker.

2. In a bowl, mix remaining ingredients together, except cilantro and chopped peanuts.

3. Cover and cook on Low 8–9 hours, or until chicken is cooked through but not dry.

4. Skim off any fat. Remove chicken to a platter and serve topped with sauce. Sprinkle with peanuts and cilantro, if you wish.

5. Serve over cooked rice.

Variation:

Vegetarians can substitute 2 (15-oz.) cans of white beans, and perhaps some tempeh, for the chicken.

Boneless Honey Mustard Chicken

Jean Halloran, Green Bay, WI

Makes 8 servings

Prep Time: 15 minutes ⚬ *Cooking Time: 3–7 hours* ⚬ *Ideal slow-cooker size: 5-qt.*

8 boneless, skinless chicken breast halves

1½ cups honey mustard dressing

½ cup water

1. Spray the inside of your slow cooker with non-stick cooking spray.

2. Cut chicken into approximately 2" pieces. Place in the slow cooker.

3. In a bowl, mix together the dressing and water. Pour over the chicken pieces.

4. Cover and cook on High 3–4 hours, or on Low 6–7 hours.

TIP

If you prefer a slightly milder flavor, add another ¼ cup water to Step 3.

That's Amore Chicken Cacciatore

Carol Sherwood, Batavia, NY

Makes 6 servings
Prep Time: 20 minutes & Cooking Time: 7–9 hours & Ideal slow-cooker size: 6-qt.

6 boneless, skinless chicken breast halves, *divided*

28-oz. jar spaghetti sauce

2 green peppers, chopped

1 onion, minced

2 Tbsp. minced garlic

1. Place a layer of chicken in your slow cooker.

2. Mix remaining ingredients together in a bowl. Spoon half of the sauce over the first layer of chicken.

3. Add remaining breast halves. Top with remaining sauce.

4. Cover and cook on Low 7–9 hours, or until chicken is tender but not dry.

5. Serve with cooked spaghetti or linguine.

Chicken in Piquant Sauce

Beth Shank, Wellman, IA
Karen Waggoner, Joplin, MO
Carol Armstrong, Winston, OR
Lois Niebauer, Pedricktown, NJ
Jean Butzer, Batavia, NY
Veronica Sabo, Shelton, CT
Charlotte Shaffer, East Earl, PA

Makes 4–6 servings
Prep Time: 10–15 minutes ॰ Cooking Time: 3–4 hours ॰ Ideal slow-cooker size: 3- to 4-qt.

16-oz. jar Russian or Creamy French salad dressing

12-oz. jar apricot preserves

1 (1.4-oz.) envelope dry onion soup mix

4–6 boneless, skinless chicken breast halves

1. In a bowl, mix together the dressing, preserves, and dry onion soup mix.

2. Place the chicken breasts in your slow cooker.

3. Pour the sauce over top of the chicken.

4. Cover and cook on High 3 hours, or on Low 4 hours, or until chicken is tender but not dry.

Variations:

1. Serve over cooked brown rice. Top individual servings with broken cashews.

—Crystal Brunk, Singers Glen, VA

2. Substitute K.C. Masterpiece BBQ Sauce with Hickory Brown Sugar for the salad dressing. Add 1 cup pineapple chunks and/or 1 cup mandarin oranges, with or without juice, to Step 1.

—Jane Hershberger, Newton, KS

3. Drop the salad dressing and use 2 12-oz. jars apricot preserves. And substitute ham or turkey for the chicken breasts.

—Shirley Sears, Sarasota, FL
—Jennifer Eberly, Harrisonburg, VA
—Marcia S. Myer, Manheim, PA

Chicken, Sweet Chicken

Anne Townsend, Albuquerque, NM

Makes 6–8 servings
Prep Time: 15 minutes ⚜ *Cooking Time: 5–6 hours* ⚜ *Ideal slow-cooker size: 3-qt.*

2 medium-sized raw sweet potatoes, peeled and cut into ¼" thick slices

8 boneless, skinless chicken thighs

8-oz. jar orange marmalade

¼ cup water

¼–½ tsp. salt

½ tsp. pepper

1. Place sweet potato slices in slow cooker.

2. Rinse and dry chicken pieces. Arrange on top of the potatoes.

3. Spoon marmalade over the chicken and potatoes.

4. Pour water over all. Season with salt and pepper.

5. Cover and cook on High 1 hour, and then turn to Low and cook 4–5 hours, or until potatoes and chicken are both tender.

Sweet and Sour Chicken

Kay Kassinger, Port Angeles, WA

Makes 6 servings
Prep Time: 15 minutes   ⚬   Cooking Time: 8–10 hours   ⚬   Ideal slow-cooker size: 3-qt.

2–3 lb. boneless, skinless chicken thighs, approximately 12 pieces

14-oz. can pineapple chunks in juice

Medium-sized yellow onion, chopped

1¼ cups bottled sweet–and–sour sauce

Garlic salt to taste

Pepper to taste

¼ cup water, *optional*

1. Spray slow cooker with non-stick cooking spray.

2. Layer chicken in slow cooker. Pour pineapple chunks and juice over chicken. Spread onion over pineapple.

3. Pour sweet–and–sour sauce over all. Sprinkle with garlic salt and pepper. If you'd like plenty of sauce, add water.

4. Cover and cook on Low 8–10 hours, or until chicken is tender, but not dry.

TIP
Wonderful served over jasmine rice.

Chicken à la Orange

Carlene Horne, Bedford, NH

Makes 8 servings
Prep Time: 7 minutes ❧ *Cooking Time: 4–6 hours* ❧ *Ideal slow-cooker size: 4-qt.*

8 boneless, skinless chicken breast halves
½ cup chopped onion
12-oz. jar orange marmalade
½ cup Russian dressing
1 Tbsp. dried parsley, or to taste

1. Place chicken and onion in slow cooker.

2. Combine marmalade and dressing. Pour over chicken.

3. Sprinkle with parsley.

4. Cover. Cook on Low 4–6 hours.

5. Serve with rice.

Orange Glazed Chicken Breasts

Corinna Herr, Stevens, PA
Karen Ceneviva, New Haven, CT

Makes 6 servings
Prep Time: 15 minutes ⚜ *Cooking Time: 4–9 hours* ⚜ *Ideal slow-cooker size: 4-qt.*

12 oz. orange juice concentrate, undiluted and thawed

½ tsp. dried marjoram leaves

6 boneless, skinless chicken breast halves

Salt and pepper to taste

¼ cup water

2 Tbsp. cornstarch

1. Combine thawed orange juice and marjoram in shallow dish. Dip each breast in orange juice mixture.

2. Sprinkle each breast with salt and pepper; then place in slow cooker. Pour remaining orange sauce over breasts.

3. Cover and cook on Low 6½–8½ hours, or on High 3½–4½ hours, or until chicken is tender but not dry.

4. Half an hour before serving, remove chicken breasts from slow cooker and keep warm on a platter.

5. Mix water and cornstarch together in a small bowl until smooth. Turn slow cooker to High. Stir cornstarch water into liquid in slow cooker.

6. Place cover slightly ajar on slow cooker. Cook until sauce is thickened and bubbly, about 15–30 minutes. Serve sauce over chicken.

Chicken Chow Mein

Clara Yoder Byler, Hartville, OH

Makes 5–6 servings

Prep Time: 30 minutes ♣ Cooking Time: 4–5 hours ♣ Ideal slow-cooker size: 4-qt.

1 lb. boneless, skinless chicken breasts, or thighs, cubed

2 cups diced celery

1 cup diced onion

2 Tbsp. soy sauce

2 cups water

¼ tsp. salt, *optional*

½ tsp. pepper, *optional*

1 Tbsp. cornstarch

¼ cup water

1. Place chicken in slow cooker. Add celery, onion, soy sauce, 2 cups water, and salt and pepper, if you wish.

2. Cover and cook on High 4 hours.

3. Just before serving, mix cornstarch with ¼ cup water in a small bowl. When smooth, add to slow cooker to thicken the sauce a bit. Heat for a few more minutes.

4. I like to serve this over cooked rice, or chow mein noodles, or both.

Pacific Chicken

Colleen Konetzni, Rio Rancho, NM

Makes 6 servings
Prep Time: 10 minutes & Cooking Time: 7–8 hours & Ideal slow-cooker size: 3- to 4-qt.

6–8 skinless chicken thighs

½ cup soy sauce

2 Tbsp. brown sugar

2 Tbsp. grated fresh ginger

2 garlic cloves, minced

1. Wash and dry chicken. Place in slow cooker.

2. Combine remaining ingredients. Pour over chicken.

3. Cover. Cook on High 1 hour. Reduce heat to Low and cook 6–7 hours.

4. Serve over rice with a fresh salad.

Simple Chicken

Norma Grieser, Clarksville, MI

Makes 8–10 servings
Prep Time: 10 minutes   ⚬   Cooking Time: 4–8 hours   ⚬   Ideal slow-cooker size: 5- to 6-qt.

½ cup water

4 lb. boneless, skinless chicken breasts

Garlic salt

1¾ cups (14 oz.) barbecue sauce

1. Put water in bottom of slow cooker. Layer in chicken pieces, sprinkling each layer with garlic salt.

2. Pour barbecue sauce over all.

3. Cover and cook on Low 8 hours, or on High 4 hours, until chicken is tender but not dry or mushy.

TIPS

1. You can add slices of onion to each layer if you wish.

2. You can use legs and thighs in place of breasts, if you wish.

Chicken Made Easy

Colleen Heatwole, Burton, MI

Makes 4–6 servings
Prep. Time: 15 minutes ❧ Cooking Time: 4 hours ❧ Ideal slow-cooker size: 4-qt.

6 boneless, skinless chicken thighs

1 envelope dry onion soup mix

1 cup reduced–fat sour cream

14¾-oz. can cream of chicken soup

1. Grease interior of slow cooker. You can use cooking spray.

2. Place chicken in slow cooker. If you need to make second layer, stagger pieces so they don't directly overlap each other.

3. In a bowl combine dry soup mix, sour cream, and chicken soup until well mixed.

4. Pour over chicken, making sure all pieces are covered.

5. Cover. Cook on Low 4 hours or until instant–read thermometer registers 165°F when inserted in center of thighs.

Serving suggestion:
Serve with rice or noodles.

Italian Chicken

Starla Kreider, Mohrsville, PA

Makes 4 servings
Prep Time: 5 minutes ⚜ *Cooking Time: 2½–8 hours* ⚜ *Ideal slow-cooker size: 3-qt.*

4 boneless, skinless chicken breast halves

28-oz. jar spaghetti sauce, your choice of special seasonings and ingredients

4 oz. shredded mozzarella cheese

1. Place the chicken in your slow cooker.

2. Pour spaghetti sauce over chicken.

3. Cover and cook on High 2½–3½ hours, or on Low 6–8 hours

4. Place chicken on serving platter and sprinkle with cheese.

5. Serve with cooked rice or spaghetti.

Zesty Italian Chicken

Yvonne Kauffman Boettger, Harrisonburg, VA

Makes 4–6 servings
Prep Time: 5 minutes ❧ Cooking Time: 4–8 hours ❧ Ideal slow-cooker size: 4-qt.

2–3 lb. boneless, skinless chicken breasts, cut into chunks

16-oz. bottle Italian dressing

¼ cup Parmesan cheese

1. Place chicken in bottom of slow cooker and pour dressing over chicken. Stir together gently.

2. Sprinkle cheese on top.

3. Cover and cook on High for 4 hours, or on Low for 8 hours, or until chicken is tender but not dry.

4. Serve over cooked rice, along with extra sauce from the chicken.

Easy Slow-Cooker Italian Chicken

Gwendolyn Muholland, Corryton, TN

Makes 4–6 servings

Prep. Time: 5–20 minutes ⚜ *Cooking Time: 4–8 hours* ⚜ *Ideal slow-cooker size: 4-qt.*

2–3 boneless, skinless chicken breasts

23½-oz. jar Prego Traditional Italian sauce

14½-oz. jar Prego Homestyle Alfredo sauce

1 cup shredded mozzarella cheese

16-oz. box pasta

1. Place the uncooked chicken breasts in the bottom of the slow cooker.

2. Top with Italian sauce, Alfredo sauce, and shredded mozzarella.

3. Cover and cook on Low for 6–8 hours or High for 4 hours.

4. When you're ready to eat, cook pasta according to the directions on the package.

5. Serve chicken on top of pasta with sauce.

TIP
Cook pasta right before serving, or cook it the night before and warm it up before serving.

Bacon–Feta Stuffed Chicken

Tina Goss, Duenweg, MO

Makes 4 servings
Prep Time: 10 minutes ❧ *Cooking Time: 1½–3 hours* ❧ *Ideal slow-cooker size: 3-qt.*

¼ cup crumbled cooked bacon

¼ cup crumbled feta cheese

4 boneless, skinless chicken
breast halves

2 (14½-oz.) cans diced tomatoes

1 Tbsp. dried basil

1. In a small bowl, mix bacon and cheese together lightly.

2. Cut a pocket in the thicker side of each chicken breast. Fill each with ¼ of the bacon and cheese. Pinch shut and secure with toothpicks.

3. Place chicken in slow cooker. Top with tomatoes and sprinkle with basil.

4. Cover and cook on High 1½–3 hours, or until chicken is tender, but not dry or mushy.

Apricot Stuffing and Chicken

Elizabeth Colucci, Lancaster, PA

Makes 5 servings

Prep. Time: 10 minutes   ❧   *Cooking Time: 2–3½ hours*   ❧   *Ideal slow-cooker size: 5-qt.*

1 stick (8 Tbsp.) butter, *divided*

1 box cornbread stuffing mix

4 boneless, skinless chicken breast halves

6–8-oz. jar apricot preserves

1. In a mixing bowl, make stuffing using ½ stick (4 Tbsp.) butter and amount of water called for in instructions on box. Set aside.

2. Cut up chicken into 1-inch pieces. Place on bottom of slow cooker. Spoon stuffing over top.

3. In microwave or on stovetop, melt remaining ½ stick (4 Tbsp.) butter with preserves. Pour over stuffing.

4. Cover and cook on High for 2 hours, or on Low for 3½ hours, or until chicken is tender but not dry.

Chicken and Stuffing

Karen Waggoner, Joplin, MO

Makes 4 servings
Prep Time: 5 minutes & *Cooking Time: 2–2½ hours* & *Ideal slow-cooker size: 4-qt.*

4 boneless, skinless chicken breast halves

6-oz. box stuffing mix for chicken

16-oz. pkg. frozen whole-kernel corn

Half a stick (4 Tbsp.) butter, melted

2 cups water

1. Place chicken in bottom of slow cooker.

2. Mix remaining ingredients together in a mixing bowl. Spoon over chicken.

3. Cover and cook on High 2–2½ hours, or until chicken is tender and the stuffing is dry.

Uncle Tim's Chicken and Sauerkraut

Tim Smith, Rutledge, PA

Makes 4 servings

Prep Time: 30 minutes   Cooking Time: 5–8 hours   Ideal slow-cooker size: 3½-qt.

4 large boneless, skinless chicken breast halves

1-lb. bag sauerkraut

12-oz. can beer

8 medium-sized red potatoes, washed and quartered

Salt and pepper to taste

Water

1. Place chicken in slow cooker.

2. Spoon sauerkraut over chicken.

3. Pour beer into slow cooker.

4. Add potatoes. Sprinkle generously with salt and pepper.

5. Pour water over all until everything is just covered.

6. Cover and cook on High for 5 hours, or on Low for 8 hours, or until chicken and potatoes are tender, but not dry.

Quickie Barbecued Chicken

Carol Sherwood, Batavia, NY
Sharon Shank, Bridgewater, VA

Makes 4 servings
Prep Time: 20 minutes ⚭ Cooking Time: 3–7 hours ⚭ Ideal slow-cooker size: 4-qt.

4 boneless, skinless chicken breast halves

¾ cup chicken broth

1 cup barbecue sauce

1 medium-sized onion, sliced

Salt and pepper to taste

1. Place all ingredients in slow cooker. Stir gently.

2. Cook on High 3 hours, or on Low 6–7 hours, or until chicken is tender but not dry.

3. Serve the breast pieces whole, or cut up and stir through the sauce.

Curried Chicken Dinner

Janessa Hochstedler, East Earl, PA

Makes 6 servings
Prep Time: 20 minutes   Cooking Time: 5–10 hours   Ideal slow-cooker size: 3-qt.

1 ½ lb. boneless, skinless chicken thighs, quartered

3 potatoes, peeled and cut into chunks, about 2 cups

1 apple, chopped

2 Tbsp. curry powder

14½-oz. can chicken broth

1 medium-sized onion, chopped, *optional*

1. Place all ingredients in slow cooker. Mix together gently.

2. Cover and cook on Low 8–10 hours or on High 5 hours, or until chicken is tender, but not dry.

3. Serve over cooked rice.

Chicken Curry with Rice

Jennifer Yoder Sommers, Harrisonburg, VA

Makes 6 servings
Prep Time: 10 minutes   Cooking Time: 5–10 hours   Ideal slow-cooker size: 3- to 4-qt.

1½ lb. boneless, skinless chicken thighs, quartered

1 onion, chopped

2 cups uncooked, long-grain rice

2 Tbsp. curry powder

14½-oz. can chicken broth

1. Combine all ingredients in your slow cooker.

2. Cover and cook on Low 8–10 hours, or on High 5 hours, or until chicken is tender but not dry.

Variation:

Add 1 chopped apple to Step 1. Thirty minutes before the end of the cooking time, stir in 2 cups frozen peas.

Sweet 'N' Sour Chicken with Veggies

Jennifer Eberly, Harrisonburg, VA

Makes 6 servings

Prep Time: 10 minutes ⚬ *Cooking Time: 8–10 hours* ⚬ *Ideal slow-cooker size: 3½- to 4-qt.*

2 lb. boneless, skinless chicken thighs (about 12), cut into 1½" pieces

25–28-oz. jar sweet–and–sour simmer sauce

1-lb. pkg. San Francisco vegetables (frozen broccoli, carrots, water chestnuts, and red peppers), thawed

1. Combine chicken chunks and cooking sauce in slow cooker.

2. Cover and cook on Low 8–10 hours, or until chicken is tender and no longer pink.

3. Ten minutes before serving, stir in vegetables. Cover and increase heat to High. Cook 10 minutes, or until vegetables are crisp-tender.

4. Serve over hot cooked rice

Teriyaki Chicken

Elaine Vigoda, Rochester, NY

Makes 6 servings
Prep Time: 15 minutes   Cooking Time: 5–6 hours   Ideal slow-cooker size: 5-qt.

1 lb. boneless, skinless chicken thighs, cut into chunks

1 lb. boneless, skinless chicken breasts, cut into large chunks

10-oz. bottle teriyaki sauce

½ lb. snow peas, optional

8-oz. can water chestnuts, drained, *optional*

1. Place chicken in slow cooker. Cover with sauce. Stir until sauce is well distributed.

2. Cover and cook on Low 4–5 hours, or until chicken is tender. Add snow peas and water chestnuts, if you wish.

3. Cover and cook another hour on Low.

4. Serve over cooked white rice or Chinese rice noodles.

Mushroom Chicken

Brenda Pope, Dundee, OH

Makes 4 servings
Prep. Time: 5 minutes ❧ Cooking Time: 8 hours ❧ Ideal slow-cooker size: 4-qt.

1 lb. boneless, skinless chicken breasts

1 .87-oz. pkg. dry chicken gravy mix

10¾-oz. can cream of mushroom, or chicken, soup

1 cup white wine

8-oz. pkg. cream cheese, softened

1. Put chicken in slow cooker. Sprinkle gravy mix on top. In separate bowl, combine soup and wine and pour over gravy mix.

2. Cover. Cook on Low 8 hours.

3. During last 30 minutes of cooking time, stir in cream cheese. Before serving, remove chicken (keeping it warm) and whisk the sauce until smooth.

Serving suggestion:

Serve chicken and sauce over noodles or rice.

10 Ingredients or Fewer

Frances's Roast Chicken

Frances Schrag, Newton, KS

Makes 6 servings
Prep. Time: 5–10 minutes ❧ *Cooking Time: 4–10 hours* ❧ *Ideal slow-cooker size: 4- to 5-qt.*

3–4-lb. whole frying chicken

Salt and pepper to taste

½ tsp. poultry seasoning

Half an onion, chopped

1 rib celery, chopped

¼ tsp. dried basil

1. Sprinkle chicken cavity with salt, pepper, and poultry seasoning. Put onion and celery inside cavity. Put chicken in slow cooker. Sprinkle with basil.

2. Cover. Cook on Low 8–10 hours, or on High 4–6 hours.

Chicken in a Pot

Carolyn Baer, Conrath, WI
Evie Hershey, Atglen, PA
Judy Koczo, Plano, IL
Mary Puskar, Forest Hill, MD
Mary Wheatley, Mashpee, MA

Makes 6 servings
Prep. Time: 10 minutes 🐦 Cooking Time: 3½–10 hours 🐦 Ideal slow-cooker size: 5-qt.

2 carrots, sliced

2 onions, sliced

2 celery ribs, cut in 1-inch pieces

2 potatoes, peeled and sliced

3 lb. chicken, whole, or cut up

2 tsp. salt

½ tsp. dried coarse black pepper

1 tsp. dried basil

½ cup water, or chicken broth, or white cooking wine

1. Place vegetables in bottom of slow cooker. Place chicken on top of vegetables. Add seasonings and water.

2. Cover. Cook on Low 8–10 hours, or on High 3½–5 hours (use 1 cup liquid if cooking on High).

NOTE
This is a great foundation for soups, such as chicken vegetable and chicken noodle.

California Chicken

Shirley Sears, Tiskilwa, IL

Makes 4–6 servings
Prep. Time: 10 minutes ♣ Cooking Time: 8½–9½ hours ♣ Ideal slow-cooker size: 4-qt.

3-lb. chicken, quartered
1 cup orange juice
⅓ cup chili sauce
2 Tbsp. soy sauce
1 Tbsp. molasses
1 tsp. dry mustard
1 tsp. garlic salt
3 medium oranges, peeled and separated into slices, or 13½-oz. can mandarin oranges

1. Arrange chicken in slow cooker.

2. In separate bowl, combine juice, chili sauce, soy sauce, molasses, dry mustard, and garlic salt. Pour over chicken.

3. Cover. Cook on Low 8–9 hours.

4. Stir in oranges. Heat 30 minutes longer.

Variation:

Stir 1 tsp. curry powder in with sauces and seasonings. Stir 1 small can pineapple chunks and juice in with oranges. Garnish with chopped green onions.

Cherry Chicken

Hope Comerford, Clinton Township, MI

Makes 4–6 servings
Prep. Time: 5 minutes & Cooking Time: 7–8 hours & Ideal slow-cooker size: 4-qt.

4 chicken leg quarters

2 cups whole cherries, pitted, then chopped

¼ cup sugar

1 small onion, halved and sliced

1 tsp. salt

1 tsp. garlic powder

¼ tsp. pepper

1. Place chicken leg quarters in crock.

2. In a bowl, mix together the remaining ingredients. Pour this over the chicken in the crock.

3. Cover and cook on Low for 7–8 hours.

Honeyed Chicken

Christie Anne Detamore–Hunsberger, Harrisonburg, VA

Makes 4–5 servings
Prep Time: 15 minutes ♣ *Cooking Time: 4–5 hours* ♣ *Ideal slow-cooker size: 3- to 4-qt.*

2 Tbsp. butter

½ cup honey

¼ cup prepared mustard

¼ tsp. salt

I tsp. curry powder

I whole chicken, cut up, or 4–5 good-sized chicken breast halves

1. Melt butter in saucepan.

2. Add honey, mustard, salt, and curry. Mix together well.

3. Place chicken in slow cooker.

4. Spoon liquid mixture over each piece of chicken.

5. Cover. Cook on Low 4–5 hours, or just until chicken is tender.

Greek Chicken

Judy Govotsus, Monrovia, MD

Makes 4–6 servings
Prep. Time: 10 minutes ♣ *Cooking Time: 5–10 hours* ♣ *Ideal slow-cooker size: 6-qt.*

4–6 potatoes, quartered
2–3 lb. chicken pieces
2 large onions, quartered
1 whole bulb garlic, minced
3 tsp. dried oregano
1 tsp. salt
½ tsp. pepper
1 Tbsp. olive oil

1. Place potatoes in bottom of slow cooker. Add chicken, onions, and garlic. Sprinkle with seasonings. Top with oil.

2. Cover. Cook on High 5–6 hours, or on Low 9–10 hours.

Lemon Garlic Chicken

Cindy Krestynick, Glen Lyon, PA

Makes 4 servings
Prep. Time: 15 minutes ⚬ *Cooking Time: 2½–5½ hours* ⚬ *Ideal slow-cooker size: 2-qt.*

1 tsp. dried oregano

½ tsp. seasoned salt

¼ tsp. pepper

2 lb. chicken breast halves, skinned and rinsed

2 Tbsp. butter, or margarine

¼ cup water

3 Tbsp. lemon juice

2 garlic cloves, minced

1 tsp. chicken bouillon granules

1 tsp. minced fresh parsley

1. Combine oregano, salt, and pepper. Rub all of mixture into chicken. Brown chicken in butter or margarine in skillet. Transfer to slow cooker.

2. Place water, lemon juice, garlic, and bouillon granules in skillet. Bring to boil, loosening browned bits from skillet. Pour over chicken.

3. Cover. Cook on High 2–2½ hours, or on Low 4–5 hours.

Chicken and Vegetables

Jeanne Heyerly, Chenoa, IL

Makes 2 servings
Prep. Time: 10 minutes   ♣   Cooking Time: 8–9 hours   ♣   Ideal slow-cooker size: 4-qt.

2 medium potatoes, quartered

2–3 carrots, sliced

2 frozen chicken breasts, or 2 frozen drumstick/thigh pieces

Salt and pepper to taste

1 medium onion, chopped

2 garlic cloves, minced

1–2 cups shredded cabbage

16-oz. can chicken broth

1. Place potatoes and carrots in slow cooker. Layer chicken on top. Sprinkle with salt, pepper, onion, and garlic. Top with cabbage. Carefully pour chicken broth around edges.

2. Cover. Cook on Low 8–9 hours.

Chicken with Vegetables in Gravy

Trudy Kutter, Corfu, NY

Makes 4 servings

Prep Time: 20–40 minutes ⚬ *Cooking Time: 8 hours* ⚬ *Ideal slow-cooker size: 5-qt.*

2–3 cups potatoes, cubed

2–3 cups baby carrots

1 medium onion, chopped

4 bone-in chicken breast halves

2 (.87-oz.) pkgs. dry chicken gravy mix

1 cup water

1 tsp. thyme

Scant tsp. poultry seasoning

1 cup sour cream, or condensed cream soup

1. Place vegetables in slow cooker. Stir together until well mixed.

2. Put chicken on top of vegetables.

3. Mix dry gravy mix with water, thyme, and poultry seasoning in a medium bowl.

4. Pour gravy into slow cooker.

5. Cook on Low 8 hours, or until vegetables and chicken are tender and done to your liking.

6. Remove meat and vegetables to serving platter.

7. Whisk sour cream or cream soup into broth.

8. Pour over chicken and vegetables and serve.

Cranberry Chicken

Teena Wagner, Waterloo, ON

Makes 6–8 servings
Prep. Time: 5–10 minutes ♣ *Cooking Time: 4–8 hours* ♣ *Ideal slow-cooker size: 4- to 5-qt.*

3–4 lb. chicken pieces
½ tsp. salt
¼ tsp. pepper
½ cup diced celery
½ cup diced onions
16-oz. can whole-berry cranberry sauce
1 cup barbecue sauce

1. Combine all ingredients in slow cooker.

2. Cover. Bake on High for 4 hours, or on Low for 6–8 hours.

Chicken with Tropical Barbecue Sauce

Lois Stoltzfus, Honey Brook, PA

Makes 6 servings
Prep. Time: 5 minutes ⚬ *Cooking Time: 3–9 hours* ⚬ *Ideal slow-cooker size: 4-qt.*

¼ cup molasses

2 Tbsp. cider vinegar

2 Tbsp. Worcestershire sauce

2 tsp. prepared mustard

⅛–¼ tsp. hot pepper sauce

2 Tbsp. orange juice

3 whole chicken breasts, halved

1 small onion, peeled and sliced

1. Combine molasses, vinegar, Worcestershire sauce, mustard, hot pepper sauce, and orange juice. Brush over chicken.

2. Place chicken in slow cooker. Add onions and stir.

3. Cover. Cook on Low 7–9 hours, or on High 3–4 hours.

Sweet Aromatic Chicken

Anne Townsend, Albuquerque, NM

Makes 4 servings
Prep. Time: 5 minutes ⚜ *Cooking Time: 5–6 hours* ⚜ *Ideal slow-cooker size: 4-qt.*

½ cup coconut milk
½ cup water
8 chicken thighs, skinned
½ cup brown sugar
2 Tbsp. soy sauce
⅛ tsp. ground cloves
2 garlic cloves, minced

1. Combine coconut milk and water. Pour into greased slow cooker.

2. Add remaining ingredients in order listed.

3. Cover. Cook on Low 5–6 hours.

Tasty Drumsticks

Trudy Kutter, Corfu, NY

Makes 5–6 servings
Prep Time: 20 minutes ⚶ Cooking Time: 6 hours ⚶ Ideal slow-cooker size: 5-qt.

3–4 lb. chicken drumsticks, skin removed
8-oz. can tomato sauce
¼ cup soy sauce
¼ cup brown sugar
1 tsp. minced garlic
3 Tbsp. cornstarch
¼ cup cold water

1. Place drumsticks in slow cooker.

2. Combine tomato sauce, soy sauce, brown sugar, and garlic in a bowl.

3. Pour over drumsticks, making sure that each drumstick is sauced.

4. Cover. Cook on Low 6 hours, or until chicken is tender.

5. Remove chicken with tongs to a platter and keep it warm.

6. Strain juices into saucepan.

7. In a bowl combine cornstarch and water until smooth.

8. Add cornstarch mixture to saucepan.

9. Bring mixture to a boil, stirring continuously.

10. Stir for two minutes until thickened.

Serving suggestion:
Serve sauce alongside, or spooned over, chicken.

TIP
The sauce is also a tasty dip for sides, such as fries.

Garlic and Lemon Chicken

Hope Comerford, Clinton Township, MI

Makes 5 servings
Prep. Time: 5 minutes & Cooking Time: 5–6 hours & Ideal slow-cooker size: 3- or 5-qt.

4–5 lb. boneless, skinless chicken breasts or thighs

½ cup minced shallots

½ cup olive oil

¼ cup lemon juice

1 Tbsp. garlic paste (or use 1 medium clove garlic, minced)

1 Tbsp. no-salt seasoning

⅛ tsp. pepper

1. Place chicken in slow cooker.

2. In a small bowl, mix the remaining ingredients. Pour this mixture over the chicken in the crock.

3. Cover and cook on Low for 5–6 hours.

Balsamic Chicken

Hope Comerford, Clinton Township, MI

Makes 4 servings
Prep. Time: 10 minutes   Cooking Time: 5–6 hours   Ideal slow-cooker size: 3-qt.

2 lb. boneless, skinless chicken breasts

2 Tbsp. olive oil

½ tsp. salt

½ tsp. pepper

1 onion, halved and sliced

28-oz. can diced tomatoes

½ cup balsamic vinegar

2 tsp. sugar

2 tsp. garlic powder

2 tsp. Italian seasoning

Cooked pasta for serving

1. Place chicken in crock. Drizzle with olive oil and sprinkle with salt and pepper.

2. Spread the onion over the top of the chicken.

3. In a bowl, mix together the diced tomatoes, balsamic vinegar, sugar, garlic powder, and Italian seasoning. Pour this over the chicken and onions.

4. Cover and cook on Low for 5–6 hours.

5. Serve over cooked pasta.

Darla's Chicken Cacciatore

Darla Sathre, Baxter, MN

Makes 6 servings
Prep. Time: 5–10 minutes ⚶ *Cooking Time: 8 hours* ⚶ *Ideal slow-cooker size: 4-qt.*

2 onions, thinly sliced
4 boneless chicken breasts, cubed
3 garlic cloves, minced
¼ tsp. pepper
2 tsp. dried oregano
1 tsp. dried basil
1 bay leaf
2 (15-oz.) cans diced tomatoes
8-oz. can tomato sauce
4-oz. can sliced mushrooms

1. Place onions in bottom of slow cooker. Add remaining ingredients.

2. Cover. Cook on Low 8 hours.

Serving suggestion:
Serve over hot spaghetti.

Chicken Cacciatore

Donna Lantgen, Arvada, CO

Makes 6 servings
Prep Time: 10 minutes ❦ *Cooking Time: 5–6 hours* ❦ *Ideal slow-cooker size: 5-qt.*

I green pepper, chopped
I onion, chopped
I Tbsp. Italian seasoning
15½-oz. can tomatoes, chopped
½ cup tomato juice
6 boneless, skinless chicken breast halves

1. Mix green pepper, onion, Italian seasoning, tomatoes, and tomato juice in a bowl.

2. Spread ½ cup of mixture over bottom of slow cooker.

3. Place 3 chicken breast pieces on top of vegetable mixture.

4. Spoon half the remaining vegetable mixture over those pieces.

5. Add remaining 3 pieces of meat.

6. Pour remaining mixture over chicken.

7. Cook on Low 5–6 hours, or until chicken is cooked through, but isn't dry or mushy.

Serving suggestion:

Serve topped with grated mozzarella or Parmesan cheese.

Chicken Parmigiana

Brenda Pope, Dundee, OH

Makes 6 servings
Prep. Time: 10–15 minutes   ♣   Cooking Time: 6¼–8¼ hours   ♣   Ideal slow-cooker size: 4-qt.

1 egg
1 tsp. salt
¼ tsp. pepper
6 boneless, skinless chicken breast halves
1 cup Italian bread crumbs
2–4 Tbsp. butter
14-oz. jar pizza sauce
6 slices mozzarella cheese
Grated Parmesan cheese

1. Beat egg, salt, and pepper together. Dip chicken into egg and coat with bread crumbs. Sauté chicken in butter in skillet. Arrange chicken in slow cooker.

2. Pour pizza sauce over chicken.

3. Cover. Cook on Low 6–8 hours.

4. Layer mozzarella cheese over top and sprinkle with Parmesan cheese. Cook an additional 15 minutes.

Creamy Italian Chicken

Jo Zimmerman, Lebanon, PA

Makes 6 servings
Prep. Time: 10 minutes ♣ Cooking Time: 4 hours ♣ Ideal slow-cooker size: 3-qt.

2 lb. chicken tenders

1 .7-oz. envelope Italian
salad dressing mix

¼ cup water

8-oz. pkg. cream cheese

1 can cream of chicken soup

1 can of mushrooms drained, *optional*

1. Place chicken in slow cooker.

2. Combine dressing mix and water. Pour over chicken.

3. Cover and cook on Low 3 hours.

4. Beat cream cheese and soup together and stir in mushrooms if you like. Pour over chicken and cook 1 hour longer.

Serving suggestion:

Serve over rice.

Creamy Chicken Italiano

Sharon Easter, Yuba City, CA
Rebecca Meyerkorth, Wamego, KS
Bonnie Miller, Cochranville, PA

Makes 4 servings
Prep. Time: 5 minutes ♣ Cooking Time: 4 hours ♣ Ideal slow-cooker size: 4-qt.

4 boneless, skinless chicken breast halves

1 envelope dry Italian salad dressing mix

¼ cup water

8-oz. pkg. cream cheese, softened

10¾-oz. can cream of chicken soup

4-oz. can mushroom stems and pieces, drained

1. Place chicken in slow cooker.

2. Combine salad dressing mix and water. Pour over chicken.

3. Cover. Cook on Low 3 hours.

4. Combine cheese and soup until blended. Stir in mushrooms. Pour over chicken.

5. Cover. Cook on Low 1 hour, or until chicken juices run clear.

Serving suggestion:

Serve over noodles or rice.

Slow-Cooker Tex–Mex Chicken

Kim Stoltzfus, Parkesburg, PA

Makes 4–6 servings
Prep Time: 15–20 minutes ⚜ *Cooking Time: 3–8 hours* ⚜ *Ideal slow-cooker size: 3½-qt.*

1 lb. boneless, skinless chicken breasts, cut into ¾-inch-wide strips

2 Tbsp. dry taco seasoning mix

2 Tbsp. flour

1 green pepper, cut into strips

1 red pepper, cut into strips

1 cup frozen corn

1½ cups chunky salsa

1. Toss chicken with seasoning and flour in slow cooker.

2. Gently stir in vegetables and salsa.

3. Cook on Low 6–8 hours, or on High 3–4 hours, until chicken and vegetables are cooked through but are not dry or mushy.

4. Stir before serving.

Serving suggestion:

Serve topped with shredded Mexican–style cheese.

Slow-Cooker Chicken Fajitas

Lisa Clark, Chesterfield, MI

Makes 6–8 servings
Prep. Time: 20 minutes ⚬ Cooking Time: 3–8 hours ⚬ Ideal slow-cooker size: 3-qt.

2 lb. skinless, boneless breasts

2 peppers, sliced (red, green, or yellow)

1 large onion, sliced

1 envelope taco seasoning

10-oz. can Ro*Tel® or plain diced tomatoes

Juice of 1 lime

1. Place half of the peppers and onions on bottom of crock.

2. Place chicken breasts on top of veggies.

3. Sprinkle taco seasoning on both sides of breasts.

4. Place remaining peppers and onions on top of chicken.

5. Pour tomatoes over top.

6. Squeeze lime juice over top. Cover and cook on Low 7–8 hours or High 3–4 hours.

7. If you prefer, you can shred chicken before serving or serve sliced.

Serving suggestion:

This pairs well with white rice, Spanish rice, or refried beans.

Slow-Cooker Chicken and Salsa

Marcia S. Myer, Manheim, PA

Makes 6 servings
Prep. Time: 10 minutes ❧ Cooking Time: 4–10 hours ❧ Ideal slow-cooker size: 5-qt.

2 (15-oz.) cans black beans

1½ lb. boneless chicken breasts, cut into serving–size pieces

16-oz. jar black bean salsa

16 oz. corn salsa

1 cup uncooked brown rice

2 cups water

1 cup sour cream

1 cup shredded cheddar cheese or Mexican blend cheese

1 avocado, sliced, for garnish

½ (5-oz.) pkg. corn chips, for garnish

1. Combine the beans, chicken, black bean salsa, corn salsa, brown rice, and 2 cups water in a slow cooker.

2. Cook on High for 4 hours or on Low for 8–10 hours, adding water if needed near the end of the cooking time.

3. To serve, place 1½ cups of the chicken mixture on individual serving plates. Top with the sour cream and cheese. Garnish with the avocado and corn chips.

Salsa Ranch Chicken with Black Beans

Hope Comerford, Clinton Township, MI

Makes 8–10 servings
Prep. Time: 5 minutes ☙ Cooking Time: 5–6 hours ☙ Ideal slow-cooker size: 5-qt.

2–3 lb. boneless, skinless chicken breasts

1¼-oz. pkg. taco seasoning

1-oz. pkg. dry ranch dressing mix

1 cup salsa

10¾ oz. can cream of chicken soup

15½ oz. can black beans, drained and rinsed

1. Place the chicken in the bottom of your crock.

2. In a bowl, mix together the taco seasoning, ranch dressing mix, salsa, cream of chicken soup, and black beans. Pour it over the chicken.

3. Cover and cook on Low for 5–6 hours.

4. Remove the chicken and shred it between two forks. Replace the chicken back in the crock and stir.

Serving suggestions:

This is great in tacos, on nachos, on top of a salad, on top of rice, or just on its own!

TIP
To make this even more delicious, include a dollop of sour cream and some shredded cheese when serving. Black olives and sliced green onions make a nice accompaniment as well.

Easy Enchilada Shredded Chicken

Hope Comerford, Clinton Township, MI

Makes 10–14 servings
Prep. Time: 5 minutes ⚭ Cooking Time: 5–6 hours ⚭ Ideal slow-cooker size: 3- or 5-qt.

5–6 lb. boneless, skinless
chicken breast

14.5-oz. can petite diced tomatoes

1 medium onion, chopped

8 oz. red enchilada sauce

½ tsp. salt

½ tsp. chili powder

½ tsp. basil

½ tsp. garlic powder

¼ tsp. pepper

1. Place chicken in the crock.

2. Add in the remaining ingredients.

3. Cover and cook on Low for 5–6 hours.

4. Remove chicken and shred it between two forks. Place the shredded chicken back in the crock and stir to mix in the juices.

Serving suggestion:

Serve over salad, brown rice, quinoa, sweet potatoes, nachos, or soft shell corn tacos. Add a dollop of yogurt and a sprinkle of fresh cilantro.

Jazzed-Up Barbecue Pulled Chicken

Hope Comerford, Clinton Township, MI

Makes 6–8 servings
Prep. Time: 5 minutes & Cooking Time: 6–7 hours & Ideal slow-cooker size: 4-qt.

2 lb. boneless, skinless chicken breasts

1 cup ketchup

¼ cup molasses

2 Tbsp. apple cider vinegar

2 Tbsp. Worcestershire sauce

1 clove garlic, minced

2 tsp. dry mustard

2 Tbsp. orange juice

1 tsp. orange zest

1. Place chicken in crock.

2. In a bowl, mix together the ketchup, molasses, apple cider vinegar, Worcestershire sauce, minced garlic, mustard powder, orange juice, and orange zest. Pour over the chicken.

3. Cover and cook on Low for 6–7 hours.

4. Remove the chicken and shred between two forks, then stir back through the sauce in the crock.

Serving suggestion:

Serve on buns with your favorite toppings.

Juicy Orange Chicken

Andrea Maher, Dunedin, FL

Makes 6 servings
Prep. Time: 10 minutes ♣ *Cooking Time: 6–8 hours* ♣ *Ideal slow-cooker size: 5- or 6-qt.*

18–24 oz. boneless, skinless chicken breast, cut into small pieces

1 cup orange juice, no additives

¼ cup honey

6 small oranges, peeled and sliced

¼ cup Bragg's liquid aminos

6 cups broccoli slaw

1. Add all the ingredients to the slow cooker except the broccoli slaw.

2. Cover and cook on High 3–4 hours or Low 6–8 hours.

3. Divide mixture between 6 mason jars.

4. Add 1 cup broccoli slaw to each mason jar.

5. Pour into a bowl when you're ready to eat or serve over salad!

Chicken Sweet and Sour

Willard E. Roth, Elkhart, IN

Makes 8 servings

Prep. Time: 10 minutes ❧ *Cooking Time: 6½ hours* ❧ *Ideal slow-cooker size: 4- to 5-qt.*

4 medium potatoes, sliced

8 boneless, skinless chicken breast halves

2 Tbsp. cider vinegar

¼ tsp. ground nutmeg

I tsp. dry basil, or I Tbsp. chopped fresh basil

2 Tbsp. brown sugar

I cup orange juice

Dried parsley flakes

17-oz. can water–pack sliced peaches, drained

1. Place potatoes in greased slow cooker. Arrange chicken on top.

2. In separate bowl, combine vinegar, nutmeg, basil, brown sugar, and orange juice. Pour over chicken. Sprinkle with parsley.

3. Cover. Cook on Low 6 hours.

4. Remove chicken and potatoes from sauce and arrange on warm platter.

5. Turn cooker to High. Add peaches and heat until warm.

Serving suggestion:

Spoon peaches and sauce over chicken and potatoes. Garnish with fresh parsley and orange slices.

Chicken with Spicy Sesame Sauce

Colleen Heatwole, Burton, MI

Makes 6–8 servings

Prep. Time: 20 minutes ❧ Cooking Time: 4 hours ❧ Ideal slow-cooker size: 4-qt.

6 boneless, skinless chicken breast thighs

¼ cup finely chopped onion

2 Tbsp. tahini (sesame paste)

1 tsp. red wine vinegar

2 cloves garlic, minced

1 tsp. gingerroot, finely shredded

2 Tbsp. soy sauce

1. Spray slow cooker with cooking spray.

2. Place chicken breast halves on bottom of slow cooker, trying to overlap as little as possible.

3. Soften finely chopped onion with 2 Tbsp. water in the microwave.

4. Combine softened onions, tahini, red wine vinegar, minced garlic, gingerroot, and soy sauce.

5. Pour over chicken and spread sauce evenly.

6. Cook until internal temperature of chicken is 165°F on instant–read thermometer when inserted into thickest part of thighs, about 4 hours on Low.

Serving suggestions:

This sauce works fabulously to drizzle over potatoes or rice. Chicken can also be shredded for sandwiches with sauce added so it isn't dry.

TIP

Drain chicken and place on platter, reserving sauce. A Microplane works best for shredding the gingerroot.

Asian Style Chicken with Pineapple

Andrea Maher, Dunedin, FL

Makes 6 servings
Prep. Time: 10 minutes ❧ *Cooking Time: 6–8 hours* ❧ *Ideal slow-cooker size: 5- or 6-qt.*

24 oz. boneless, skinless chicken breast cut into bite size pieces

3 cups pineapple, cubed

¼ cup Bragg's liquid aminos

1 Tbsp. brown sugar

½ cup chopped onion or 2 Tbsp. onion powder

1 cup low-sodium gluten–free chicken broth or stock

½ tsp. ground ginger

2 16-oz. bags frozen Szechuan mixed veggies or any mixed veggies

1. Add all ingredients except for frozen veggies to the slow cooker.

2. Cover and cook on High 3–4 hours or Low 6–8 hours.

3. Add frozen veggies in the last 1–2 hours.

Chicken and Egg Noodles

Janie Steele, Moore, OK

Makes 5–7 servings
Prep. Time: 15 minutes ⚜ *Cooking Time: 5–6 hours* ⚜ *Ideal slow-cooker size: 5-qt.*

1 14-oz. can low-sodium cream of chicken soup

2 (15½-oz.) cans low-sodium chicken broth

1 tsp. garlic powder

1 tsp. onion powder

¼ tsp. celery seed

¼ tsp. pepper

4 Tbsp. butter or margarine

1 lb. boneless, skinless chicken breasts

24-oz. bag frozen egg noodles

1. Place all ingredients in crock except the noodles.

2. Cover and cook for 5–6 hours on Low.

3. Remove chicken and shred. Return to slow cooker, then add frozen noodles and cook for an additional 40–60 minutes, or until noodles are tender.

Slow-Cooker Chicken and Dumplings

Kris Zimmerman, Lititz, PA

Makes 8–10 servings
Prep. Time: 15 minutes & Cooking Time: 5–7 hours & Ideal slow-cooker size: 5-qt.

4–6 boneless, skinless chicken breasts

2 Tbsp. butter, melted

2 (10½-oz.) cans cream of chicken soup

1 onion, diced

14-oz. can chicken broth

1 Tbsp. dried parsley

16.3-oz. pkg. Pillsbury Grands! Biscuits

1. Place chicken breasts, butter, soup, onion, chicken broth, and parsley in crock.

2. Cover and cook on High for 4–6 hours.

3. After 4–6 hours, break chicken up using 2 forks or tongs.

4. Cut biscuits into small pieces. Kitchen shears work great for this.

5. Stir biscuits into chicken and cook on High for an additional 40–50 minutes.

11 Ingredients or More

Savory Slow-Cooker Chicken

Sara Harter Fredette, Williamsburg, MA

Makes 4 servings

Prep. Time: 10–15 minutes   ❧   *Cooking Time: 8–10 hours*   ❧   *Ideal slow-cooker size: 4- to 5-qt.*

2½ lb. chicken pieces, skinned

1 lb. fresh tomatoes, chopped, or 15-oz. can stewed tomatoes

2 Tbsp. white wine

1 bay leaf

¼ tsp. pepper

2 garlic cloves, minced

1 onion, chopped

½ cup chicken broth

1 tsp. dried thyme

1½ tsp. salt

2 cups broccoli, cut into bite-sized pieces

1. Combine all ingredients except broccoli in slow cooker.

2. Cover. Cook on Low 8–10 hours.

3. Add broccoli 30 minutes before serving.

Braised Chicken with Summer Tomatoes

Karen Ceneviva, Seymour, CT

Makes 6 servings
Prep Time: 30 minutes ⚜ *Cooking Time: 3–4 hours* ⚜ *Ideal slow-cooker size: 6-qt.*

4½-lb. chicken, cut into 8 pieces (excluding back and wings; save them for making soup another day)

Salt and pepper to taste

4 Tbsp. extra virgin olive oil, *divided*

1 large yellow onion, chopped

10 cloves garlic, peeled

½ cup wine vinegar

1½ cups chicken broth

4 fresh tarragon sprigs, or 2 Tbsp. finely chopped fresh tarragon leaves

6–8 medium (about 3½ lb.) tomatoes, chopped

1. Season chicken to taste with salt and pepper.

2. Place 2 Tbsp. oil in large skillet. Brown chicken, a few pieces at a time, over medium–high heat in skillet. Turn once and brown underside.

3. When both sides of each piece of chicken are browned, remove from skillet and keep warm on platter.

4. Add 2 Tbsp. oil to skillet. Stir in chopped onion. Sauté over medium heat about 8 minutes.

5. Add garlic and sauté about 5 minutes. Add vinegar and broth and simmer 1 minute.

6. Carefully pour oil/vinegar/ onion/garlic mixture into slow cooker. Place chicken on top.

7. Tuck tarragon sprigs around chicken pieces, or sprinkle with chopped tarragon. Spoon chopped tomatoes over top.

8. Cover. Cook on Low 3–4 hours.

Chicken Vegetable Dish

Cheri Jantzen, Houston, TX

Makes 4 servings
Prep. Time: 10 minutes & Cooking Time: 5–7 hours & Ideal slow-cooker size: 4- to 5-qt.

4 skinless chicken breast halves,
with bone in

15-oz. can crushed tomatoes

10-oz. pkg. frozen green beans

2 cups water, or chicken broth

1 cup brown rice, uncooked

1 cup sliced mushrooms

2 carrots, chopped

1 onion, chopped

½ tsp. minced garlic

½ tsp. herb-blend seasoning

¼ tsp. dried tarragon

1. Combine all ingredients in slow cooker.

2. Cover. Cook on High 2 hours, and then on Low 3–5 hours.

Ann's Chicken Cacciatore

Ann Driscoll, Albuquerque, NM

Makes 6–8 servings
Prep. Time: 10 minutes ⚹ Cooking Time: 3–9 hours ⚹ Ideal slow-cooker size: 4-qt.

1 large onion, thinly sliced

2½–3-lb. chicken, cut up

2 (6-oz.) cans tomato paste

4-oz. can sliced mushrooms, drained

1 tsp. salt

¼ cup dry white wine

¼ tsp. pepper

1–2 garlic cloves, minced

1–2 tsp. dried oregano

½ tsp. dried basil

½ tsp. celery seed, *optional*

1 bay leaf

1. Place onion in slow cooker. Add chicken.

2. Combine remaining ingredients. Pour over chicken.

3. Cover. Cook on Low 7–9 hours, or on High 3–4 hours.

Serving suggestion:

Serve over spaghetti.

Fruited Barbecue Chicken

Barbara Katrine Rose, Woodbridge, VA

Makes 4–6 servings
Prep. Time: 5 minutes   Cooking Time: 4 hours   Ideal slow-cooker size: 4-qt.

29-oz. can tomato sauce

20-oz. can unsweetened crushed
pineapple, undrained

2 Tbsp. brown sugar

3 Tbsp. vinegar

1 Tbsp. instant minced onion

1 tsp. paprika

2 tsp. Worcestershire sauce

¼ tsp. garlic powder

⅛ tsp. pepper

3 lb. chicken, skinned and cubed

11-oz. can mandarin oranges, drained

1. Combine all ingredients except chicken and oranges. Add chicken pieces.

2. Cover. Cook on High 4 hours.

3. Just before serving, stir in oranges.

Serving suggestion:

Serve over hot rice.

Marcy's Barbecued Chicken

Marcy Engle, Harrisonburg, VA

Makes 6 servings

Prep. Time: 5–7 minutes ⚶ *Cooking Time: 5 hours* ⚶ *Ideal slow-cooker size: 4-qt.*

2 lb. chicken pieces

¼ cup flour

1 cup ketchup

2 cups water

⅓ cup Worcestershire sauce

1 tsp. chili powder

½ tsp. salt

½ tsp. pepper

2 drops Tabasco sauce

¼ tsp. garlic salt

¼ tsp. onion salt

1. Dust chicken with flour. Transfer to slow cooker.

2. Combine remaining ingredients. Pour over chicken.

3. Cover. Cook on Low 5 hours.

Orange Chicken and Sweet Potatoes

Kimberlee Greenawalt, Harrisonburg, VA

Makes 6 servings
Prep. Time: 10 minutes ⚹ Cooking Time: 3–10 hours ⚹ Ideal slow-cooker size: 4-qt.

2–3 sweet potatoes, peeled and sliced

3 whole chicken breasts, halved

⅔ cup flour

I tsp. salt

I tsp. nutmeg

½ tsp. cinnamon

Dash pepper

Dash garlic powder

10¾-oz. can cream of celery, or cream of chicken, soup

4-oz. can sliced mushrooms, drained

½ cup orange juice

½ tsp. grated orange rind

2 tsp. brown sugar

3 Tbsp. flour

1. Place sweet potatoes in bottom of slow cooker.

2. Rinse chicken breasts and pat dry. Combine flour, salt, nutmeg, cinnamon, pepper, and garlic powder. Thoroughly coat chicken in flour mixture. Place on top of sweet potatoes.

3. Combine soup with remaining ingredients. Stir well. Pour over chicken breasts.

4. Cover. Cook on Low 8–10 hours, or on High 3–4 hours.

Serving suggestion:

Serve over rice.

Orange Chicken Leg Quarters

Kimberly Jensen, Bailey, CO

Makes 4–5 servings

Prep. Time: 15 minutes ❧ Cooking Time: 6–7 hours ❧ Ideal slow-cooker size: 5- to 6-qt.

4 chicken drumsticks

4 chicken thighs

1 cup strips of green and red bell peppers

½ cup canned chicken broth

½ cup prepared orange juice

½ cup ketchup

2 Tbsp. soy sauce

1 Tbsp. light molasses

1 Tbsp. prepared mustard

½ tsp. garlic salt

11-oz. can mandarin oranges

2 tsp. cornstarch

1 cup frozen peas

1. Place chicken in slow cooker. Top with pepper strips.

2. Combine broth, juice, ketchup, soy sauce, molasses, mustard, and garlic salt. Pour over chicken.

3. Cover. Cook on Low 6–7 hours.

4. Remove chicken and vegetables from slow cooker. Keep warm.

5. Measure out 1 cup of cooking sauce. Put in saucepan and bring to boil.

6. Drain oranges, reserving 1 Tbsp. juice. Stir cornstarch into reserved juice. Add to boiling sauce in pan.

7. Add peas to sauce and cook, stirring for 2–3 minutes until sauce thickens and peas are warm. Stir in oranges.

Serving suggestion:

Arrange chicken pieces on platter of cooked white rice, fried cellophane noodles, or lo mein noodles. Pour orange sauce over chicken and rice or noodles. Top with sliced green onions.

Sweet and Sour Chicken

Bernice A. Esau, North Newton, KS

Makes 6 servings
Prep. Time: 10 minutes & Cooking Time: 8–10 hours & Ideal slow-cooker size: 4½-qt.

1 ½ cups sliced carrots

1 large green pepper, chopped

1 medium onion, chopped

2 Tbsp. quick-cooking tapioca

2½–3-lb. chicken,
cut into serving–size pieces

8-oz. can pineapple chunks in juice

⅓ cup brown sugar

⅓ cup vinegar

1 Tbsp. soy sauce

½ tsp. instant chicken bouillon

¼ tsp. garlic powder

¼ tsp. ground ginger, or ½ tsp. freshly
grated ginger

1 tsp. salt

1. Place vegetables in bottom of slow cooker. Sprinkle with tapioca. Add chicken.

2. In separate bowl, combine pineapple, brown sugar, vinegar, soy sauce, bouillon, garlic powder, ginger, and salt. Pour over chicken.

3. Cover. Cook on Low 8–10 hours.

Serving suggestion:

Serve over cooked rice.

Honey Balsamic Chicken

Hope Comerford, Clinton Township, MI

Makes 4–6 servings
Prep. Time: 5 minutes & *Cooking Time: 7–8 hours* & *Ideal slow-cooker size: 5- or 6-qt.*

4 cups chopped red potatoes

1½ tsp. kosher salt, *divided*

1 tsp. pepper, *divided*

8–10 boneless, skinless chicken thighs

1 cup sliced red onion

1 pint cherry tomatoes

½ cup balsamic vinegar

¼ cup honey

2 Tbsp. olive oil

¼ tsp. red pepper flakes

½ tsp. dried thyme

½ tsp. dried rosemary

3 cloves garlic, minced

3 cups green beans

1. Spray crock with non-stick cooking spray.

2. Place potatoes in bottom of crock. Sprinkle with ½ tsp. of salt and ½ tsp. pepper.

3. Place chicken and onion on top of potatoes and pour cherry tomatoes over the top.

4. Mix together the balsamic vinegar, honey, olive oil, 1 tsp. salt, remaining ½ tsp. pepper, red pepper flakes, thyme, rosemary, and garlic. Pour this mixture over the chicken, tomatoes, and potatoes.

5. Cook on Low for 7–8 hours, or until potatoes are tender.

6. 20–30 minutes before serving, add the green beans on top.

Chicken Mole

Bernadette Veenstra, Grand Rapids, MI

Makes 8 servings

Prep. Time: 30 minutes ❧ *Cooking Time: 4–5 hours* ❧ *Ideal slow-cooker size: 6-qt.*

1 Tbsp. olive oil

8–10 chicken thighs, skinned and lightly salted and peppered

1 large onion, peeled and chopped

4–6 garlic cloves, minced

4 tsp. chili powder

4 tsp. unsweetened cocoa powder

¼ tsp. cinnamon

2½ cups gluten–free chicken broth or stock

2 Tbsp. natural creamy peanut butter

2 Tbsp. tomato paste

½ cup dark raisins

4 cups cooked brown rice

½ cup loosely packed cilantro leaves

Lime wedges

1. Heat olive oil in a large skillet. In several batches, brown all sides of chicken (about 10 minutes total).

2. Place chicken in bottom of slow cooker lightly coated with cooking spray. Discard all but 1 Tbsp. of pan drippings.

3. Heat pan drippings or oil in same skillet. Add onion and cook, stirring until softened (about 5 minutes). Add garlic, chili powder, cocoa powder, and cinnamon to skillet and cook, stirring 1 minute.

4. Stir in broth, peanut butter, tomato paste, and raisins.

5. Pour sauce over chicken in slow cooker.

6. Cook on Low for 4–5 hours, or until chicken registers 165°F on meat thermometer.

7. Serve over cooked brown rice and garnish with cilantro and lime wedges.

Chicken Marsala

Hope Comerford, Clinton Township, MI

Makes 4–6 servings
Prep. Time: 35 minutes & Cooking Time: about 5½ hours & Ideal slow-cooker size: 4-qt.

½ cup cornstarch

1 tsp. salt

½ tsp. pepper

1 tsp. oregano

½ cup or so of olive oil, *divided*

4 lb. thinly sliced boneless, skinless chicken breasts

1 large onion, halved and sliced into half–rings

2¼ cups Marsala wine, *divided*

1½ Tbsp. butter

12 oz. baby bella (a.k.a. portobello) mushrooms, sliced

½ cup milk

1. In a casserole dish, mix together the cornstarch, salt, pepper, and oregano.

2. Heat about ¼ cup of the olive oil in a large frying pan over medium heat.

3. Coat each side of your chicken breasts with the cornstarch mixture and place them in the frying pan until each side is slightly browned.

4. Place each breast into the crock.

5. In the same pan you just browned the chicken, add about 1½ Tbsp. olive oil and sauté the onions until they are just slightly translucent. Add in 2 cups of Marsala wine and cook on high heat for about 7 minutes, or until it thickens. Pour it over the chicken in the crock.

6. Cover and cook on Low for 4½ hours.

7. Over medium-high heat, melt the butter and remaining 1½ Tbsp. olive oil. Add in the mushrooms and cook for about 5 minutes.

8. Add in the remaining ¼ cup Marsala wine and whisk in the ½ cup milk. (Whisking will keep it from curdling.)

9. Pour the mushroom mixture over the chicken and cover and cook an additional 30 minutes.

Coq au Vin

Kimberlee Greenawalt, Harrisonburg, VA

Makes 6 servings
Prep. Time: 10–15 minutes ⚜ *Cooking Time: 6¼–8¼ hours* ⚜ *Ideal slow-cooker size: 4- to 5-qt.*

2 cups frozen pearl onions, thawed

4 thick slices bacon, fried and crumbled

1 cup sliced button mushrooms

1 garlic clove, minced

1 tsp. dried thyme leaves

⅛ tsp. black pepper

6 boneless, skinless chicken breast halves

½ cup dry red wine

¾ cup chicken broth

¼ cup tomato paste

3 Tbsp. flour

1. Layer ingredients in slow cooker in the following order: onions, bacon, mushrooms, garlic, thyme, pepper, chicken, wine, and broth.

2. Cover. Cook on Low 6–8 hours.

3. Remove chicken and vegetables. Cover and keep warm.

4. Ladle ½ cup cooking liquid into small bowl. Cool slightly. Turn slow cooker to High. Cover. Mix reserved liquid, tomato paste, and flour until smooth. Return mixture to slow cooker, cover, and cook 15 minutes, or until thickened.

Serving suggestion:

Serve chicken, vegetables, and sauce over noodles.

Chicken Casablanca

Joyce Kaut, Rochester, NY

Makes 6–8 servings

Prep. Time: 30 minutes   ❧   Cooking Time: 4½–6½ hours   ❧   Ideal slow-cooker size: 4- to 5-qt.

2 large onions, sliced

1 tsp. ground ginger

3 garlic cloves, minced

2 Tbsp. oil

3 large carrots, diced

2 large potatoes, diced

3 lb. skinless chicken pieces

½ tsp. ground cumin

½ tsp. salt

½ tsp. pepper

¼ tsp. cinnamon

2 Tbsp. raisins

14½-oz. can chopped tomatoes

3 small zucchini, sliced

15-oz. can garbanzo beans, drained

2 Tbsp. chopped parsley

1. Sauté onions, ginger, and garlic in oil in skillet. (Reserve oil.) Transfer vegetables to slow cooker. Add carrots and potatoes.

2. Brown chicken over medium heat in reserved oil. Transfer to slow cooker. Mix gently with vegetables.

3. Combine seasonings in separate bowl. Sprinkle over chicken and vegetables. Add raisins and tomatoes.

4. Cover. Cook on High 4–6 hours.

5. Add sliced zucchini, beans, and parsley 30 minutes before serving.

Serving suggestion:

Serve over cooked rice or couscous.

Variation:

Add ½ tsp. turmeric and ¼ tsp. cayenne pepper to Step 3.

—Michelle Mann, Mt. Joy, PA

Autumn Chicken and Veggies

Nanci Keatley, Salem, OR

Makes 6 servings

Prep Time: 20 minutes ⚬ *Cooking Time: 4–6 hours* ⚬ *Ideal slow-cooker size: 6-qt.*

2 yellow onions, chopped

2 parsnips, cut into $\frac{1}{2}$-inch-thick slices

3 carrots, cut into $\frac{1}{2}$-inch-thick slices

1 lb. celery root, cut into chunks

$\frac{1}{2}$ tsp. salt

$\frac{1}{4}$–$\frac{1}{2}$ tsp. pepper

6 boneless chicken breast halves

Salt and pepper to taste

1 tsp. tarragon

1 cup chicken broth

$\frac{1}{2}$ cup white wine

1. Place vegetables in slow cooker. Stir in salt and pepper. Mix well.

2. Lay chicken pieces over vegetables.

3. Season with salt and pepper. Sprinkle with tarragon.

4. Pour broth and wine around the chicken pieces, so as not to disturb the seasonings.

5. Cover. Cook on Low 4–6 hours, or until vegetables and chicken are tender and done to your liking.

Serving suggestion:

Serve with mashed potatoes or some good French bread.

Stuffed Chicken Rolls

Lois M. Martin, Lititz, PA
Renee Shirk, Mount Joy, PA

Makes 6 servings
Prep. Time: 25 minutes ⚜ Refrigeration Time: 1 hour ⚜ Cooking Time: 4–5 hours ⚜ Ideal slow-cooker size: 4-qt.

6 large boneless, skinless chicken breast halves

6 slices fully cooked ham

6 slices Swiss cheese

¼ cup flour

¼ cup grated Parmesan cheese

½ tsp. rubbed sage

¼ tsp. paprika

¼ tsp. pepper

¼ cup oil

10¾-oz. can cream of chicken soup

½ cup chicken broth

1. Flatten chicken to ⅛–inch thickness. Place ham and cheese slices on each breast. Roll up and tuck in ends. Secure with toothpick.

2. Combine flour, Parmesan cheese, sage, paprika, and pepper. Coat chicken on all sides. Cover and refrigerate for 1 hour.

3. Brown chicken in oil in skillet. Transfer to slow cooker.

4. Combine soup and broth. Pour over chicken.

5. Cover. Cook on Low 4–5 hours.

Melanie's Chicken Cordon Bleu

Melanie Thrower, McPherson, KS

Makes 6 servings
Prep. Time: 15 minutes ⚬ *Cooking Time: 4–5 hours* ⚬ *Ideal slow-cooker size: 4-qt.*

3 whole chicken breasts,
split and deboned

6 pieces thinly sliced ham

6 slices Swiss cheese

Salt and pepper to taste

6 slices bacon

¼ cup water

1 tsp. chicken bouillon granules

½ cup white cooking wine

1 tsp. cornstarch

¼ cup cold water

1. Flatten chicken to ⅛- to ¼-inch thickness. Place a slice of ham and a slice of cheese on top of each flattened breast. Sprinkle with salt and pepper. Roll up and wrap with strip of bacon. Secure with toothpick. Place in slow cooker.

2. Combine ¼ cup water, granules, and wine. Pour into slow cooker.

3. Cover. Cook on High 4 hours.

4. Combine cornstarch and ¼ cup cold water. Add to slow cooker. Cook until sauce thickens.

Chicken Curry

Maricarol Magill, Freehold, NJ

Makes 4 servings

Prep. Time: 10 minutes   ❧   Cooking Time: 5¼–6¼ hours   ❧   Ideal slow-cooker size: 5-qt.

4 boneless, skinless chicken breast halves

1 small onion, chopped

2 sweet potatoes (about 1½ lb.), cubed

⅔ cup orange juice

1 garlic clove, minced

1 tsp. chicken bouillon granules

1 tsp. salt

¼ tsp. pepper

4 tsp. curry powder

2 Tbsp. cornstarch

2 Tbsp. cold water

Toppings:

Sliced green onions

Shredded coconut

Peanuts

Raisins

1. Place chicken in slow cooker. Cover with onions and sweet potatoes.

2. Combine orange juice, garlic, chicken bouillon granules, salt, pepper, and curry powder. Pour over vegetables.

3. Cover. Cook on Low 5–6 hours.

4. Remove chicken and vegetables and keep warm.

5. Turn slow cooker to High. Dissolve cornstarch in cold water. Stir into sauce in slow cooker. Cover. Cook on High 15–20 minutes.

Serving suggestion:

Serve chicken and sauce over rice. Sprinkle with your choice of toppings.

Barbara's Creole Chicken

Barbara McGinnis, Jupiter, FL

Makes 4 servings
Prep. Time: 15 minutes   ❧   *Cooking Time: 6 hours*   ❧   *Ideal slow-cooker size: 4½-qt.*

2 (.9-oz.) pkgs. dry béarnaise sauce mix

½ cup dry white wine

1 lb. boneless, skinless chicken breasts, cut into bite-sized cubes

9-oz. pkg. frozen mixed vegetables

1 lb. cooked ham, cubed

1 lb. red potatoes, cubed

1 red bell pepper, chopped

1 green bell pepper, chopped

3 shallots, minced

½ tsp. garlic powder

½ tsp. turmeric powder

½ tsp. dried tarragon

1. Combine all ingredients in slow cooker.

2. Cover. Cook on Low 6 hours.

Jambalaya

Hope Comerford, Clinton Township, MI

Makes 4–5 servings

Prep. Time: 20 minutes   ♣   Cooking Time: 8 hours   ♣   Ideal slow-cooker size: 3-qt.

1 lb. boneless, skinless chicken, chopped into 1–inch pieces

½ lb. Andouille sausage

1 large onion, chopped

1 green bell pepper, seeded and chopped

2 cups okra, chopped

1 rib celery, chopped

28-oz. can diced tomatoes

1 cup chicken broth

2 tsp. dried oregano

2 tsp. Cajun seasoning

1 tsp. salt

1 tsp. hot sauce

2 bay leaves

½ tsp. thyme

1 lb. frozen peeled and cooked shrimp, thawed

Cooked rice

1. Place all of the ingredients into the crock except the shrimp and rice, and stir.

2. Cover and cook on Low for 8 hours.

3. Right before you are ready to serve, add the shrimp and let cook an additional 5 minutes.

4. Serve over rice.

TIP
Make 5-minute rice while the shrimp is cooking and everything will be ready to go all at the same time!

Healthy Chicken Chow Mein

Hope Comerford, Clinton Township, MI

Makes 6 servings
Prep. Time: 15–20 minutes ⚬ Cooking Time: 6½–7½ hours ⚬ Ideal slow-cooker size: 3- or 4-qt.

2–3 large boneless, skinless chicken breasts

2 cups water

2 medium onions, halved and sliced into half rings

2–3 cups chopped celery

1 tsp. kosher salt

¼ tsp. pepper

2 tsp. quick-cooking tapioca

¼ cup low sodium soy sauce or Bragg's liquid aminos

¼ cup brown sugar

16-oz. can baby corn, drained

6.5-oz. can bamboo shoots, drained

1 cup bean sprouts

1 red bell pepper, chopped into slivers

1 carrot, chopped into thin matchsticks

1. Place the chicken breasts in the crock with the water, onions, celery, salt, and pepper.

2. Cover and cook on Low for 5–6 hours.

3. While the chicken is cooking, in a small bowl mix together the tapioca, soy sauce, and brown sugar.

4. Remove the chicken and shred it between 2 forks.

5. Mix the sauce you just made with the juices in the slow cooker. Add the chicken back in and all the remaining veggies. Stir.

6. Cook on Low an additional 1½ hours.

Serving suggestion:

Serve over Chinese or Thai rice noodles.

Garlic Mushroom Thighs

Elaine Vigoda, Rochester, NY

Makes 6 servings
Prep. Time: 15 minutes ☙ Cooking Time: 4 hours ☙ Ideal slow-cooker size: 5-qt.

3 Tbsp. all-purpose flour

6 boneless, skinless chicken thighs

8–10 garlic cloves, peeled and very lightly crushed

1 Tbsp. olive oil

¾ lb. fresh mushrooms, any combination of varieties, cut into bite-sized pieces

⅓ cup balsamic vinegar

1¼ cups chicken broth or stock

1–2 bay leaves

½ tsp. dried thyme or 4 sprigs fresh thyme

2 tsp. apricot preserves (low-sugar or no sugar added preferred)

1. Grease interior of slow cooker.

2. Place flour in a strong plastic bag without any holes. Once by one, put each thigh in bag, hold the bag shut, and shake it to flour the thigh fully.

3. Place thighs in the crock. If you need to make a second layer, stagger the pieces so they don't directly overlap.

4. If you have time, sauté the garlic in oil in skillet just until it begins to brown. Otherwise, use raw.

5. Sprinkle garlic over thighs, including those on bottom layer.

6. Scatter cut-up mushrooms over thighs too, remembering those on the bottom layer.

7. Mix remaining ingredients together in a bowl, stirring to break up the preserves.

8. When well mixed, pour into the cooker along the edges so you don't wash the vegetables off the chicken pieces.

9. Cover and cook on Low for 4 hours, or until an instant-read thermometer registers 160–165°F when stuck into the thighs.

10. Serve meat topped with vegetables with sauce spooned over.

Serving suggestion:
Serve over cooked spaghetti squash.

Cheesy Buffalo Chicken Pasta

Christina Gerber, Apple Creek, OH

Makes 6–8 servings
Prep. Time: 15 minutes ♣ Cooking Time: High for 4 hours or Low for 8 hours ♣ Ideal slow-cooker size: 6-qt.

3 cups chicken broth

½ cup buffalo wing sauce, *divided*

1 Tbsp. dry ranch dressing mix

¾ teaspoon garlic powder

½ tsp. salt

⅛ tsp. black pepper

1½ lb. boneless, skinless chicken thighs

8-oz. pkg. cream cheese, cubed

1 cup shredded sharp cheddar cheese

1 Tbsp. cornstarch plus 1 Tbsp. water

1 lb. linguine

Chopped cilantro, optional

1. Grease interior of slow-cooker crock.

2. Mix broth, ¼ cup buffalo sauce, and seasonings in crock.

3. Submerge chicken in sauce.

4. Scatter cubed cream cheese and shredded cheese over chicken.

5. Cover. Cook on Low 4 hours.

6. When chicken is fully cooked, remove to bowl and shred with 2 forks. (Cover crock to keep sauce warm.)

7. Add remaining ¼ cup buffalo sauce to shredded chicken and toss to coat. Set aside but keep warm.

8. In a small bowl, stir cornstarch and water together until smooth. Stir into warm sauce in crock until sauce smooths out and thickens.

9. Break noodles in half and place in crock.

10. Top with shredded chicken and cover.

11. Cook on High 30–60 minutes, or just until noodles are fully cooked. Stir 3–4 times during cooking.

12. If you need more liquid for noodles to cook, add water ¼ cup at a time.

13. Garnish with cilantro if you wish, and serve immediately.

TIP
This is a great one-pot meal. No extra pan needed to cook the pasta!

Chicken Lettuce Wraps

Hope Comerford, Clinton Township, MI

Makes About 12 wraps

Prep. Time: 15 minutes ⚓ *Cooking Time: 2–3 hours* ⚓ *Ideal slow-cooker size: 5- or 7-qt.*

2 lb. ground chicken, browned

4 cloves garlic, minced

½ cup minced sweet yellow onion

4 Tbsp. soy sauce or Bragg's liquid aminos

1 Tbsp. natural crunchy peanut butter

1 tsp. rice wine vinegar

1 tsp. sesame oil

¼ tsp. kosher salt

¼ tsp. red pepper flakes

¼ tsp. black pepper

8-oz. can sliced water chestnuts, drained, rinsed, chopped

3 green onions, sliced

12 good-sized pieces of iceberg lettuce, rinsed and patted dry

1. In the crock, combine the ground chicken, garlic, yellow onion, soy sauce or liquid aminos, peanut butter, vinegar, sesame oil, salt, red pepper flakes, and black pepper.

2. Cover and cook on Low for 2–3 hours.

3. Add in the water chestnuts and green onions. Cover and cook for an additional 10–15 minutes.

4. Serve a good spoonful on each piece of iceberg lettuce.

Buffalo Chicken Meatballs

Hope Comerford, Clinton Township, MI

Makes 6 servings
Prep. Time: 20–30 minutes & Cooking Time: 6 hours & Ideal slow-cooker size: 5- or 6-qt.

1½ lb. ground chicken

¾ cup hot sauce of your choice, *divided*

2 Tbsp. dry minced onion

2 Tbsp. garlic powder

¼ tsp. pepper

1 egg

1 cup panko bread crumbs

1½–2 Tbsp. coconut oil

2 tsp. chicken bouillon granules

1 cup water

2 cups non-fat plain Greek yogurt

2 Tbsp. cornstarch

1. In a bowl, combine the ground chicken, ½ cup hot sauce, minced onion, garlic powder, pepper, egg, and panko bread crumbs.

2. Heat the coconut oil in a large skillet over medium-high heat.

3. Roll the chicken mixture into 1½–2-inch balls. Place them in the skillet, turning them regularly so they're seared on each side.

4. Place the seared meatballs into your crock. Sprinkle them with the chicken bouillon granules and pour in the water.

5. Cover and cook on Low for 6 hours.

6. Remove the meatballs in a covered dish to keep them warm.

7. In a bowl, stir together the Greek yogurt, cornstarch, and remaining ¼ cup of hot sauce. Gently whisk this back into your crock with the juices.

8. You can either place your browned meatballs back into the sauce to coat them, or you can serve the meatballs with the sauce spooned over the top.

Serving suggestion:

Serve meatballs over browned rice with a fresh salad on the side. If desired, add more hot sauce to taste.

Casseroles

One–Dish Chicken Supper

Louise Stackhouse, Benton, PA

Makes 4 servings
Prep. Time: 5 minutes ♣ Cooking Time: 6–8 hours ♣ Ideal slow-cooker size: 4-qt.

4 boneless, skinless chicken breast halves

10¾-oz. can cream of chicken, or celery, or mushroom, soup

⅓ cup milk

1 6-oz. pkg. Stove Top stuffing mix and seasoning packet

1⅔ cups water

1. Place chicken in slow cooker.

2. Combine soup and milk. Pour over chicken.

3. Combine stuffing mix, seasoning packet, and water. Spoon over chicken.

4. Cover. Cook on Low 6–8 hours.

Rachel's Chicken Casserole

Maryann Markano, Wilmington, DE

Makes 6 servings
Prep Time: 25–30 minutes   ♣   Cooking Time: 4 hours   ♣   Ideal slow-cooker size: 5-qt.

2 (16-oz.) cans sauerkraut, rinsed and drained, *divided*

1 cup Light Russian salad dressing, *divided*

6 boneless, skinless chicken breast halves, *divided*

1 Tbsp. prepared mustard, *divided*

6 slices Swiss cheese

Fresh parsley for garnish, *optional*

1. Place half the sauerkraut in the slow cooker. Drizzle with ⅓ cup dressing.

2. Top with 3 chicken breast halves. Spread half the mustard on top of the chicken.

3. Top with remaining sauerkraut and chicken breasts. Drizzle with another ⅓ cup dressing. (Save the remaining dressing until serving time.)

4. Cover and cook on Low for 4 hours, or until the chicken is tender, but not dry or mushy.

5. To serve, place a breast half on each of 6 plates. Divide the sauerkraut over the chicken. Top each with a slice of cheese and a drizzle of the remaining dressing. Garnish with parsley if you wish, just before serving.

Wild Rice Hot Dish

Barbara Tenney, Delta, PA

Makes 8–10 servings
Prep. Time: 15 minutes   ♣   *Cooking Time: 4–6 hours*   ♣   *Ideal slow-cooker size: 4-qt.*

2 cups wild rice, uncooked
½ cup slivered almonds
½ cup chopped onions
½ cup chopped celery
8–12-oz. can mushrooms, drained
2 cups cut-up chicken
6 cups chicken broth
¼–½ tsp. salt
¼ tsp. pepper
¼ tsp. garlic powder
1 Tbsp. parsley

1. Wash and drain rice.

2. Combine all ingredients in slow cooker. Mix well.

3. Cover. Cook on Low 4–6 hours, or until rice is finished. Do not remove lid before rice has cooked 4 hours.

Wild Rice-Chicken-Sausage Bake

Carla Elliott, Phoenix, AZ

Makes 8–10 servings
Prep. Time: 30 minutes   ♣   *Cooking Time: 4–5 hours*   ♣   *Ideal slow-cooker size: 6-qt.*

1 lb. bulk sausage, regular, sweet Italian, or hot Italian

¾ cup uncooked wild rice

¾ cup uncooked brown rice

1 medium onion, chopped

1 cup diced celery

10.75-oz. can cream of mushroom soup

5 cups chicken broth

½ tsp. salt

½ tsp. black pepper

½ lb. fresh mushrooms, sliced, or 4-oz. can sliced mushrooms, drained

8 boneless, skinless chicken thighs

1. Brown sausage in skillet, stirring often to break up clumps, until no longer pink. Drain off drippings and discard.

2. Meanwhile, grease interior of slow-cooker crock.

3. With a slotted spoon, remove browned sausage from skillet and place in cooker.

4. Stir in uncooked wild rice and uncooked brown rice, onion, celery, cream of mushroom soup, chicken broth, salt, and pepper. Mix together well.

5. Stir in mushrooms.

6. Place thighs in cooker, pushing them down into the mixture. If you need to make a second layer, stagger the pieces so they don't directly overlap each other. Spoon some of the sauce over the top layer.

7. Cover. Cook on Low for 4 hours. Insert an instant-read meat thermometer into the thighs. If it registers 160°–165°, the chicken is finished. If it's done, remove the chicken to a large deep bowl, cover, and keep warm. If it is not, continue cooking another hour on Low, checking at the end to make sure it has reached the safe temperature.

8. Check that the rice is fully cooked. If not, it too can cook an additional hour. If the chicken is finished but the rice isn't, remove the chicken as instructed above, and allow the rice to continue cooking, covered, for another 30 minutes. Check it then. Continue cooking for 30-minute intervals and then checking, until the rice is tender.

9. To serve, place thighs in a deep bowl or platter and surround with the rice.

Chicken Reuben Bake

Gail Bush, Landenberg, PA

Makes 4 servings
Prep. Time: 5 minutes ♣ *Cooking Time: 6–8 hours* ♣ *Ideal slow-cooker size: 4-qt.*

4 boneless, skinless chicken breast halves

2-lb. bag sauerkraut, drained and rinsed

4–5 slices Swiss cheese

1¼ cups Thousand Island salad dressing

2 Tbsp. chopped fresh parsley

1. Place chicken in slow cooker. Layer sauerkraut over chicken. Add cheese. Top with salad dressing. Sprinkle with parsley.

2. Cover. Cook on Low 6–8 hours.

Chicken with Broccoli Rice

Maryann Markano, Wilmington, DE

Makes 6 servings
Prep Time: 20 minutes ⚹ *Cooking Time: 6–8 hours* ⚹ *Ideal slow-cooker size: 5-qt.*

1¼ cups uncooked long–grain rice

Pepper to taste

2 lb. boneless, skinless chicken breasts, cut into strips

1 (52 g.) pkg. Knorr's cream of broccoli dry soup mix

2½ cups chicken broth

1. Spray slow cooker with non-stick cooking spray. Place rice in cooker. Sprinkle with pepper.

2. Top with chicken pieces.

3. In a mixing bowl, combine soup mix and broth. Pour over chicken and rice.

4. Cover and cook on Low 6–8 hours, or until rice and chicken are tender but not dry.

Sweet Potato Chicken Casserole

Beverly Flatt–Getz, Warriors Mark, PA

Makes 4–6 servings
Prep Time: 20 minutes   ⚘   Cooking Time: 3–6 hours   ⚘   Ideal slow-cooker size: 3-qt.

3–4 lb. chicken, cut up
6 raw sweet potatoes, julienned
20-oz. can pineapple chunks, in juice
14½-oz. can chicken broth
2 Tbsp. cornstarch
2 Tbsp. cold water

1. Place the cut-up chicken into the slow cooker.

2. Top with sweet potatoes.

3. Pour pineapples and juice over the potatoes.

4. Then pour the chicken broth over all ingredients.

5. Cover and cook on Low for 6 hours or on High for 3 hours, or until chicken and potatoes are tender but not dry or mushy.

6. Just before serving, mix cornstarch and cold water together until smooth. Turn cooker to High. Stir cornstarch paste into cooker and cook for a few minutes until sauce thickens.

7. Place chicken and potatoes on serving dish or platter. Top with sauce.

TIP
I sprinkle chives over the chicken when I serve it.

Cheesy Chicken, Bacon, Tator Tot Slow-Cooker Bake

Kris Zimmerman, Lititz, PA

Makes 8–10 servings
Prep. Time: 15 minutes   ❧   Cooking Time: 3–4 hours   ❧   Ideal slow-cooker size: 4-qt.

32-oz. bag Tater Tots, *divided*
3 Tbsp. real bacon bits, *divided*
1 ½ cups cheddar cheese
1 ½ cups Monterey Jack cheese
5 boneless, skinless chicken breasts
Salt and pepper, to taste
¾ cup milk

1. Grease bottom of crock.

2. Layer half the Tater Tots on bottom of crock.

3. Sprinkle with 1½ Tbsp. of the bacon bits.

4. Combine the two cheeses, and sprinkle a third of it over the bacon potatoes.

5. Top cheese with chicken breasts.

6. Sprinkle chicken with salt and pepper.

7. Top chicken with another third of cheese.

8. Sprinkle with another 1½ Tbsp. of the bacon bits.

9. Add remainder of Tater Tots.

10. Top with remaining cheese.

11. Pour milk over everything.

12. Cook on High for 3–4 hours.

Green Enchiladas

Jennifer Yoder Sommers, Harrisonburg, VA

Makes 8 servings
Prep Time: 5–7 minutes ❧ *Cooking Time: 2–4 hours* ❧ *Ideal slow-cooker size: 3-qt.*

2 (10-oz.) cans green enchilada sauce, *divided*

8 large tortillas, *divided*

2 cups cooked shredded chicken, *divided*

1 ½ cups mozzarella cheese

1. Pour a little enchilada sauce on the bottom of your slow cooker.

2. Layer 1 tortilla, ¼ cup of chicken, and ¼ cup of sauce into slow cooker.

3. Repeat layers until all 3 ingredients are used completely.

4. Sprinkle mozzarella cheese over top.

5. Cover and cook on Low 2–4 hours.

TIP
Green enchilada sauce can be found in the Mexican foods section in most grocery stores.

Pre-Cooked Chicken

Chicken and Dressing

Sharon Miller, Holmesville, OH

Makes 10–12 servings
Prep. Time: 30 minutes ⚘ *Cooking Time: 4¾ hours–8¾ hours* ⚘ *Ideal slow-cooker size: 6-qt.*

12–13 cups slightly dry bread cubes
1–2 cups chopped onion
2 cups diced celery
8 Tbsp. butter, melted
1 tsp. poultry seasoning
½ tsp. dried thyme
1½ tsp. salt
½ tsp. pepper
3 cups shredded or diced
cooked chicken
3 well-beaten eggs
3½–4½ cups chicken broth

1. Place bread cubes in a large bowl.

2. Sauté onion and celery in melted butter. Stir in poultry seasoning, thyme, salt, and pepper.

3. Toss in the cooked chicken.

4. Pour entire chicken mixture over bread cubes and toss well together.

5. Add the eggs.

6. Stir in chicken broth to moisten. Pack lightly into slow cooker.

7. Cover and cook on High for 45 minutes. Reduce heat to Low and cook 4–8 hours.

Ham and Swiss Chicken

Nanci Keatley, Salem, OR
Janice Yoskovich, Carmichaels, PA

Makes 6 servings
Prep. Time: 15 minutes ⚜ *Cooking Time: 4–5 hours* ⚜ *Ideal slow-cooker size: 4-qt.*

2 eggs, beaten
1½ cups milk
2 Tbsp. butter, melted
½ cup chopped celery
¼ cup diced onion
10 slices bread, cubed
12 thin slices deli ham, rolled up
2 cups grated Swiss cheese
2½ cups cubed cooked chicken
10¾-oz. can cream of chicken soup
½ cup milk

1. Combine eggs and milk. Add butter, celery, and onion. Stir in bread cubes. Place half of mixture in greased slow cooker. Top with half the ham, cheese, and chicken.

2. Combine soup and milk. Pour half over chicken. Repeat layers.

3. Cover. Cook on Low 4–5 hours.

Mexi–Dutch Pot Pie

MarJanita Geigley, Lancaster, PA

Makes 4–5 servings
Prep. Time: 20 minutes   ♣   Cooking Time: 4 hours   ♣   Ideal slow-cooker size: 4- to 6-qt.

2 large wheat tortilla shells

10¾-oz. can reduced-sodium cream of mushroom soup

2 cups cooked, shredded chicken

4½-oz. can chopped and drained green chilies

16-oz. bag frozen mixed vegetables

⅓ cup fresh cilantro

½ tsp. minced garlic

1 cup shredded cheese

1. Spray or grease slow cooker.

2. Lay down one shell.

3. Mix other ingredients and pour on top of shell.

4. Cover with remaining shell.

5. Cover crock and cook on Low for 4 hours.

Serving suggestion:

Serve with sour cream and guacamole.

Barbecue Chicken for Buns

Linda Sluiter, Schererville, IN

Makes 16–20 servings

Prep. Time: 15 minutes   ⚶   Cooking Time: 8 hours   ⚶   Ideal slow-cooker size: 5½-qt.

6 cups diced cooked chicken
2 cups chopped celery
1 cup chopped onions
1 cup chopped green peppers
4 Tbsp. butter
2 cups ketchup
2 cups water
2 Tbsp. brown sugar
4 Tbsp. vinegar
2 tsp. dry mustard
1 tsp. pepper
1 tsp. salt

1. Combine all ingredients in slow cooker.

2. Cover. Cook on Low 8 hours.

3. Stir chicken until it shreds.

Serving suggestion:

Pile into steak rolls and serve.

Elizabeth's Hot Chicken Sandwiches

Elizabeth Yutzy, Wauseon, OH

Makes 8 servings

Prep. Time: 5 minutes   ❧   Cooking Time: 2–3 hours   ❧   Ideal slow-cooker size: 4-qt.

3 cups cubed cooked chicken

2 cups chicken broth

1 cup crushed soda crackers

¼–½ tsp. salt

Dash pepper

1. Combine chicken, broth, crackers, and seasoning in slow cooker.

2. Cover. Cook on Low 2–3 hours, until mixture thickens and can be spread.

Serving suggestion:

Fill sandwich buns and serve while warm.

Mexi Chicken Rotini

Jane Geigley, Lancaster, PA

Makes 6 servings
Prep. Time: 30 minutes & Cooking Time: 4½ hours & Ideal slow-cooker size: 4-qt.

1 cup water

3 cups partially cooked rotini

12-oz. pkg. frozen mixed vegetables

10-oz. can Ro*Tel diced tomatoes
with green chilies

4-oz. can green chilies, undrained

4 cups shredded cooked chicken

1 cup low-fat shredded cheddar cheese

1. Combine all ingredients in slow cooker except shredded cheddar.

2. Cover and cook on Low for 4 hours.

3. Top with shredded cheddar, then let cook covered an additional 20 minutes or so, or until cheese is melted.

Barbecued Chicken Pizza

Susan Roth, Salem, OR

Makes 4 to 6 servings
Prep. Time: 20–25 minutes & Cooking Time: 2½–3 hours
Standing Time: 2 hours before you begin & Ideal slow-cooker size: 6-qt.

8- or 12-oz. pkg. prepared pizza dough, depending how thick you like your pizza crust

1 cup barbecue sauce, teriyaki flavored, or your choice of flavors

2 cups cooked, chopped chicken (your own leftovers, rotisserie chicken, or canned chicken)

20-oz. can pineapple tidbits, drained, *optional*

½ cup green bell pepper, chopped, *optional*

¼ cup red onion, diced or sliced, *optional*

2 cups shredded mozzarella cheese

1. If the dough's been refrigerated, allow it to stand at room temperature for 2 hours.

2. Grease interior of slow-cooker crock.

3. Stretch the dough into a large circle so that it fits into the crock, covering the bottom and reaching up the sides by an inch or so the whole way around. (If the dough is larger than the bottom of the cooker, fold it in half and stretch it to fit the bottom and an inch up the sides. This will make a thicker crust.)

4. Bake crust, uncovered, on High 1 hour.

5. Spread barbecue sauce over hot crust.

6. Drop chopped chicken evenly over sauce.

7. If you wish, spoon pineapple, chopped peppers, and onion over chicken.

8. Sprinkle evenly with cheese.

9. Cover. Cook on High for about 2 hours, or until the crust begins to brown around the edges.

10. Uncover, being careful not to let the condensation on the lid drip onto the pizza.

11. Let stand for 10 minutes. Cut into wedges and serve.

Wings

Chili Barbecued Chicken Wings

Rosemarie Fitzgerald, Gibsonia, PA

Makes 10 full-sized servings

Prep. Time: 5 minutes ❧ Cooking Time: 2–8 hours ❧ Ideal slow-cooker size: 5-qt.

5 lb. chicken wings, tips cut off
12-oz. bottle chili sauce
⅓ cup lemon juice
1 Tbsp. Worcestershire sauce
2 Tbsp. molasses
1 tsp. salt
2 tsp. chili powder
⅓ tsp. hot pepper sauce
Dash garlic powder

1. Place wings in cooker.

2. Combine remaining ingredients and pour over chicken.

3. Cover. Cook on Low 6–8 hours, or on High 2–3 hours.

Heavenly Barbecued Chicken Wings

Tracy Supcoe, Barclay, MD

Makes 8 full-sized servings

Prep. Time: 20 minutes ⚶ *Cooking Time: 5–6 hours* ⚶ *Ideal slow-cooker size: 5-qt.*

4 lb. chicken wings

2 large onions, chopped

2 (6-oz.) cans tomato paste

2 large cloves garlic, minced

¼ cup Worcestershire sauce

¼ cup cider vinegar

½ cup brown sugar

½ cup sweet pickle relish

½ cup red or white wine

2 tsp. salt

2 tsp. dry mustard

1. Cut off wing tips. Cut wings at joint. Place in slow cooker.

2. Combine remaining ingredients. Add to slow cooker. Stir.

3. Cover. Cook on Low 5–6 hours.

Mouth–Watering Barbecued Chicken Wings

Mary L. Casey, Scranton, PA

Makes 8–12 full-sized servings
Prep. Time: 10 minutes ❧ Cooking Time: 4–6 hours ❧ Ideal slow-cooker size: 4- to 5-qt.

3–6 lb. chicken wings
1–3 Tbsp. oil
¾–1 cup vinegar
½ cup ketchup
2 Tbsp. sugar
2 Tbsp. Worcestershire sauce
3 cloves garlic, minced
1 Tbsp. dry mustard
1 tsp. paprika
½–1 tsp. salt
⅛ tsp. pepper

1. Brown wings in oil in skillet, or brush wings with oil and broil, watching carefully so they do not burn.

2. Combine remaining ingredients in slow cooker. Add wings. Stir gently so that they are all well covered with sauce.

3. Cover. Cook on Low 4–6 hours, or until tender.

Sweet Barbecue Wings

Hope Comerford, Clinton Township, MI

Makes 6–8 servings
Prep. Time: 20 minutes   ❧   Broiling Time: 16 minutes   ❧   Cooking Time: 4–5 hours
Ideal slow-cooker size: 2-qt.

3 lb. chicken wings, wing tips cut off and discarded, cut at the joint

Salt and pepper to taste

Garlic powder, to taste

12-oz. jar orange marmalade

½ cup barbecue sauce

2 Tbsp. quick–cooking tapioca

1 Tbsp. Dijon mustard

1. Preheat your oven to a low broil.

2. Put the wing pieces onto a baking sheet and sprinkle both sides with salt, pepper, and garlic powder. Put them under the broiler for 8 minutes on each side.

3. While the wings are broiling, mix together the orange marmalade, barbecue sauce, tapioca, and Dijon mustard in a small bowl.

4. When wings are browned, transfer them to your greased crock.

5. Pour the sauce over the chicken and use tongs to mix them through the sauce.

6. Cover and cook on Low for 4–5 hours.

Rosemarie's Barbecued Chicken Wings

Rosemarie Fitzgerald, Gibsonia, PA

Makes 10 full-sized servings
Prep. Time: 5 minutes ⚘ *Cooking Time: 2–8 hours* ⚘ *Ideal slow-cooker size: 5-qt.*

5 lb. chicken wings, tips cut off
12-oz. bottle chili sauce
⅓ cup lemon juice
1 Tbsp. Worcestershire sauce
2 Tbsp. molasses
1 tsp. salt
2 tsp. chili powder
¼ tsp. hot pepper sauce
Dash garlic powder

1. Place wings in cooker.

2. Combine remaining ingredients and pour over chicken.

3. Cover. Cook on Low 6–8 hours, or on High 2–3 hours.

NOTE

These wings are also a great appetizer, yielding about 15 appetizer–size servings. Take any leftover chicken off the bone and combine with leftover sauce. Serve over cooked pasta for a second meal.

Tracy's Barbecued Chicken Wings

Tracy Supcoe, Barclay, MD

Makes 8 full-sized servings

Prep. Time: 20 minutes ⚬ Cooking Time: 5–6 hours ⚬ Ideal slow-cooker size: 5-qt.

4 lb. chicken wings

2 large onions, chopped

2 (6-oz.) cans tomato paste

2 large garlic cloves, minced

¼ cup Worcestershire sauce

¼ cup cider vinegar

½ cup brown sugar

½ cup sweet pickle relish

½ cup red or white wine

2 tsp. salt

2 tsp. dry mustard

1. Cut off wing tips. Cut wings at joint. Place in slow cooker.

2. Combine remaining ingredients. Add to slow cooker. Stir.

3. Cover. Cook on Low 5–6 hours.

Mary's Chicken Wings

Mary Casey, Scranton, PA

Makes 8–12 full-sized servings
Prep. Time: 10 minutes ⚜ *Cooking Time: 4–6 hours* ⚜ *Ideal slow-cooker size: 4- to 5-qt.*

3–6 lb. chicken wings
1–3 Tbsp. oil
¾–1 cup vinegar
½ cup ketchup
2 Tbsp. sugar
2 Tbsp. Worcestershire sauce
3 garlic cloves, minced
1 Tbsp. dry mustard
1 tsp. paprika
½–1 tsp. salt
⅛ tsp. pepper

1. Brown wings in oil in skillet, or brush wings with oil and broil, watching carefully so they do not burn.

2. Combine remaining ingredients in slow cooker. Add wings. Stir gently so that they are all well covered with sauce.

3. Cover. Cook on Low 4–6 hours, or until tender.

Donna's Chicken Wings

Donna Conto, Saylorsburg, PA

Makes 10 full-sized servings

Prep. Time: 5 minutes ⚘ *Cooking Time: 3–4 hours* ⚘ *Ideal slow-cooker size: 5-qt.*

5 lb. chicken wings
28-oz. jar spaghetti sauce
1 Tbsp. Worcestershire sauce
1 Tbsp. molasses
1 Tbsp. prepared mustard
1 tsp. salt
½ tsp. pepper

1. Place wings in slow cooker.

2. Combine remaining ingredients. Pour over wings and stir them gently, making sure all are covered with sauce.

3. Cover. Cook on High 3–4 hours.

Apricot–Glazed Chicken Wings

Hope Comerford, Clinton Township, MI

Makes 8–10 servings
Prep. Time: 30 minutes ❀ Broiling Time: 16 minutes
Cooking Time: 4–6 hours ❀ Ideal slow-cooker size: 3-qt.

4 lb. chicken wings, cut at the joint, tips removed and discarded

Salt and pepper to taste

Garlic powder, to taste

12-oz. jar apricot preserves

¼ cup honey Catalina dressing

2 Tbsp. honey mustard

2 Tbsp. barbecue sauce

1 tsp. lime juice

4 dashes hot sauce

1 small onion, minced

1. Preheat your oven to a low broil.

2. Put your wing pieces onto a baking sheet and sprinkle both sides with salt, pepper, and garlic powder. Put them under the broiler for 8 minutes on each side.

3. While the wings are broiling, mix together the apricot preserves, honey Catalina dressing, honey mustard, barbecue sauce, lime juice, hot sauce, and onion.

4. When your wings are done under the broiler, place them into a greased crock.

5. Pour the sauce you just mixed over the top, then use tongs to toss the wings around to make sure they're all coated with the sauce.

6. Cook on Low for 4–6 hours.

Honey Chicken Wings

Bonnie Whaling, Clearfield, PA

Makes 6–8 servings
Prep Time: 20–30 minutes ❧ *Cooking Time: 3½–4½ hours* ❧ *Ideal slow-cooker size: 4-qt.*

3 lb. chicken wings, tips cut off, *divided*

2 Tbsp. vegetable oil

1 cup honey

½ cup soy sauce

2 Tbsp. ketchup

1. Cut each wing into two parts. Place about ⅓ of the wings in a large non-stick skillet and brown in oil. (If the skillet is crowded, the wings will not brown.) Place in slow cooker.

2. Mix remaining ingredients and pour ⅓ of the sauce over the wings in the cooker.

3. Repeat Steps 1 and 2 twice.

4. Cover and cook on High 3–4 hours, or until wings are tender but not dry.

Chicken Wings Colorado

Nancy Rexrode Clark, Woodstock, MD

Makes 6–8 servings
Prep. Time: 40 minutes & Cooking Time: 6½–7½ hours & Ideal slow-cooker size: 4-qt.

1½ cups sugar
¼ tsp. salt
1 chicken bouillon cube
1 cup cider vinegar
½ cup ketchup
2 Tbsp. soy sauce
12–16 chicken wings
¼ cup cornstarch
½ cup cold water
Red hot sauce to taste, *optional*

1. Combine sugar, salt, bouillon cube, vinegar, ketchup, and soy sauce in slow cooker. Turn to High and bring sauce to a boil.

2. Add chicken wings, pushing them down into sauce.

3. Cover. Cook on Low 6–7 hours.

4. Combine cornstarch and cold water in small bowl. Stir into slow cooker.

5. Cover. Cook on High until liquid thickens, about 30 minutes.

6. Season with red hot sauce, or let each diner add to his or her own serving.

Sweet and Sour Chicken Wings

H. Schoen, Windsor, CT

Makes 6–8 servings
Prep. Time: 15 minutes ⚜ *Cooking Time: 7 hours* ⚜ *Ideal slow-cooker size: 3- to 4-qt.*

1½ cups sugar

1 cup cider vinegar

½ cup ketchup

1 chicken bouillon cube

2 Tbsp. soy sauce

¼ tsp. salt, *optional*

¼ tsp. pepper, *optional*

16 chicken wings

¼ cup cornstarch

½ cup cold water

1. On stove in medium-sized saucepan, mix together sugar, vinegar, ketchup, bouillon cube, soy sauce, and salt and pepper if you wish.

2. Bring to a boil over medium heat. Stir to dissolve sugar and bouillon cube.

3. Put wings in slow cooker. Pour sauce over wings.

4. Cover. Simmer on Low 6½ hours, or until wings are tender but not dry.

5. A few minutes before end of cooking time, combine cornstarch and water in a small bowl. When smooth, stir gently into wings and sauce.

6. Cover. Simmer on High until liquid thickens, about 30 minutes.

7. To serve, keep cooker turned to Low. Stir occasionally.

Five-Spice Chicken Wings

Marcia Parker, Lansdale, PA

Makes 6–8 servings
Prep Time: 30 minutes ❧ *Cooking Time: 2½–5½ hours* ❧ *Ideal slow-cooker size: 3½- to 4-qt.*

3 lb. (about 16) chicken wings

1 cup bottled plum sauce (check an Asian grocery, or the Asian food aisle in a general grocery store)

2 Tbsp. butter, melted

1 tsp. five-spice powder (check an Asian grocery, or the Asian food aisle in a general grocery store)

Thinly sliced orange wedges, *optional*

Pineapple slices, *optional*

1. In a foil-lined baking pan arrange the wings in a single layer. Bake at 375° for 20 minutes. Drain well.

2. Meanwhile, combine the plum sauce, melted butter, and five-spice powder in your slow cooker. Add wings. Then stir to coat the wings with sauce.

3. Cover and cook on Low 4–5 hours, or on High 2–2½ hours.

4. Serve immediately, or keep them warm in your slow cooker on Low for up to 2 hours.

5. Garnish with orange wedges and pineapple slices to serve, if you wish.

Variation:

For Kentucky Chicken Wings, create a different sauce in Step 2. Use ½ cup maple syrup, ½ cup whiskey, and 2 Tbsp. melted butter. Then stir in the wings. Continue with Step 3.

Levi's Sesame Chicken Wings

Shirley Unternahrer, Wayland, IA

Makes 16 appetizer servings, or 6–8 main–dish servings
Prep. Time: 35–40 minutes & Cooking Time: 2½–5 hours & Ideal slow-cooker size: 4-qt.

3 lb. chicken wings

Salt and pepper to taste

1¾ cups honey

1 cup soy sauce

½ cup ketchup

2 Tbsp. canola oil

2 Tbsp. sesame oil

2 garlic cloves, minced

Toasted sesame seeds

1. Rinse wings. Cut at joint. Sprinkle with salt and pepper. Place on broiler pan.

2. Broil 5 inches from broiler flame, 10 minutes on each side. Place chicken in slow cooker.

3. Combine remaining ingredients in bowl, except sesame seeds. Pour over chicken.

4. Cover. Cook on Low 5 hours or on High 2½ hours.

5. Sprinkle sesame seeds over top just before serving.

6. Serve as appetizer, or with white or brown rice and shredded lettuce to turn this appetizer into a meal.

Soups, Stews & Chilies

Chicken Noodle Soup

Beth Shank, Wellman, IA

Makes 6–8 servings
Prep. Time: 10 minutes ⚜ *Cooking Time: 4–6 hours* ⚜ *Ideal slow-cooker size: 5-qt.*

2 tsp. chicken bouillon granules,
or 2 chicken bouillon cubes

5 cups hot water

46-oz. can chicken broth

2 cups cooked chicken

1 tsp. salt

4 cups homestyle noodles, uncooked

⅓ cup thinly sliced celery, lightly pre–
cooked in microwave

⅓ cup shredded, or chopped, carrots

1. Dissolve bouillon in water. Pour into slow cooker.

2. Add remaining ingredients. Mix well.

3. Cover. Cook on Low 4–6 hours.

Chunky Chicken Vegetable Soup

Janice Muller, Derwood, MD

Makes 6 servings
Prep Time: 20 minutes ⚜ Cooking Time: 2–6 hours ⚜ Ideal slow-cooker size: 3½- to 4-qt.

2½ cups water

8-oz. can tomato sauce

10-oz. pkg. frozen mixed vegetables, partially thawed

1½ tsp. Italian seasoning

1 (2.1-oz.) envelope dry chicken noodle soup mix

2 cups cut-up cooked chicken or turkey

1. Combine all ingredients in slow cooker.

2. Cook on Low 2–6 hours, depending upon how crunchy you like your vegetables.

Simple Chicken Rice Soup

Norma Grieser, Clarksville, MI

Makes 8 servings
Prep Time: 30 minutes & Cooking Time: 4–8 hours & Ideal slow-cooker size: 4- to 6-qt.

4 cups chicken broth

4 cups cut-up chicken, cooked

1⅓ cups cut-up celery

1⅓ cups diced carrots

1 qt. water

1 cup uncooked long–grain rice

1. Put all ingredients in slow cooker.

2. Cover and cook on Low 4–8 hours, or until vegetables are cooked to your liking.

Chicken Rice Soup

Karen Ceneviva, Seymour, CT

Makes 8 servings
Prep Time: 15 minutes & *Cooking Time: 4–8 hours* & *Ideal slow-cooker size: 3½-qt.*

½ cup wild rice, uncooked

½ cup long-grain rice, uncooked

1 tsp. vegetable oil

1 lb. boneless, skinless chicken breasts, cut into ¾–inch cubes

5¼ cups chicken broth

1 cup celery (about 2 ribs), chopped in ½–inch thick pieces

1 medium onion, chopped

2 tsp. dried thyme leaves

¼ tsp. red pepper flakes

1. Mix wild and white rice with oil in slow cooker.

2. Cover. Cook on High 15 minutes.

3. Add chicken, broth, vegetables, and seasonings.

4. Cover. Cook 4–5 hours on High or 7–8 hours on Low.

TIP

A dollop of sour cream sprinkled with finely chopped scallions on top of each individual serving bowl makes a nice finishing touch.

Mary's Chicken and Rice Soup

Becky Frey, Lebanon, PA

Makes 8–10 servings
Prep Time: 10–20 minutes ⚬ *Cooking Time: 3–4 hours* ⚬ *Ideal slow-cooker size: 3½-qt.*

4.4-oz. pkg. chicken-flavored rice and sauce

2 cups diced, cooked chicken

15-oz. can diced tomatoes and green chilies

49½-oz. can chicken broth

1. Prepare rice and sauce according to package directions.

2. Place all ingredients in slow cooker. Stir until well mixed.

3. Cover and cook on Low 3–4 hours.

TIP

1. Serve over corn chips and sprinkle with shredded cheese, if you wish.

2. If you can't find tomatoes with chilies, add a 4-oz. can of diced green chilies. Or add them anyway for extra heat.

3. You can add the rice and sauce without preparing them according to their package directions. Just stir them in uncooked, and simmer the soup an hour longer in the slow cooker, or until the rice is thoroughly cooked.

Chicken and Vegetable Soup with Rice

Hope Comerford, Clinton Township, MI

Makes 4–6 servings
Prep. Time: 20 minutes ❧ *Cooking Time: 6½–7½ hours* ❧ *Ideal slow-cooker size: 3-qt.*

1 ½–2 lb. boneless, skinless chicken breasts

1 ½ cups chopped carrots

1 ½ cups chopped red onion

2 Tbsp. garlic powder

1 Tbsp. onion powder

2 tsp. salt (you can omit the salt if you're using regular stock rather than no–salt)

¼ tsp. celery seed

¼ tsp. paprika

⅛ tsp. pepper

1 dried bay leaf

8 cups no–salt chicken stock

1 cup fresh green beans

3 cups cooked rice

1. Place chicken into the bottom of crock, then add rest of the remaining ingredients, except green beans and rice.

2. Cover and cook on Low for 6–7 hours.

3. Remove chicken and chop into bite-sized cubes. Place chicken back into crock and add in green beans. Cover and cook another 30 minutes.

4. To serve, place approximately ½ cup of the cooked rice into each bowl and ladle soup over top of the rice.

Italiano Chicken, Rice, and Tomato Soup

Jane Geigley, Lancaster, PA

Makes 6 servings
Prep. Time: 30 minutes   ⚬   Cooking Time: 4–6 hours   ⚬   Ideal slow-cooker size: 4-qt.

½ cup chopped onion

2 Tbsp. butter, softened

½ tsp. paprika

½ tsp. basil

⅛ tsp. garlic powder

8-oz. brick cream cheese, softened

1¼ cups milk

2 (10¾-oz.) cans tomato soup

2 (16-oz.) cans whole tomatoes, undrained

1 cup instant rice

2 cups cooked chopped chicken

1 cup shredded mozzarella cheese

1. In a stand mixer, mix the first 9 ingredients. Beat until smooth. Pour into the slow cooker.

2. Stir in rice and chicken.

3. Cover and cook on Low for 4–6 hours. Add the shredded cheese at the very end, just before serving.

Tasty Chicken Soup

Rhonda Freed, Lowville, NY

Makes 12 servings
Prep Time: 10–15 minutes ☙ Cooking Time: 6–7 hours ☙ Ideal slow-cooker size: 4-qt.

12 cups chicken broth

2 cups chicken, cooked and cut into small pieces

1 cup shredded carrots

3 whole cloves

Small onion

16-oz. bag of dry noodles, cooked, *optional*

1. Place broth, chicken, and carrots in slow cooker.

2. Peel onion. Using a toothpick, poke 3 holes on the cut ends. Carefully press cloves into 3 of the holes until only their round part shows. Add to slow cooker.

3. Cover and cook on High 6–7 hours.

4. If you'd like a thicker soup, add a bag of cooked fine egg noodles before serving.

TIP

You can make the broth and cook the chicken in your slow cooker, too. Just put 2–3 lb. of cut-up chicken pieces into the slow cooker. Add 12 cups water. Cook on High 4–5 hours, or until chicken is tender and falling off the bone. Remove the chicken with a slotted spoon. Debone when cooled enough to handle. Measure 2 cups of chicken meat and return to slow cooker. Completely cool the remaining chicken and freeze or refrigerate for future use. Continue with the recipe above to make the soup.

Chicken and Corn Soup

Eleanor Larson, Glen Lyon, PA

Makes 4–6 servings
Prep. Time: 15 minutes   ♣   Cooking Time: 8–9 hours   ♣   Ideal slow-cooker size: 4-qt.

2 whole boneless, skinless chicken breasts, cubed
1 onion, chopped
1 garlic clove, minced
2 carrots, sliced
2 ribs celery, chopped
2 medium potatoes, cubed
1 tsp. mixed dried herbs
⅓ cup tomato sauce
12-oz. can cream-style corn
14-oz. can whole kernel corn
3 cups chicken stock
¼ cup chopped Italian parsley
1 tsp. salt
¼ tsp. pepper

1. Combine all ingredients except parsley, salt, and pepper in slow cooker.

2. Cover. Cook on Low 8–9 hours, or until chicken is tender.

3. Add parsley and seasonings 30 minutes before serving.

Easy Chicken Tortilla Soup

Becky Harder, Monument, CO

Makes 6–8 servings

Prep. Time: 5–10 minutes ⚶ *Cooking Time: 8 hours* ⚶ *Ideal slow-cooker size: 4- to 5-qt.*

4 chicken breast halves

2 (15-oz.) cans black beans, undrained

2 (15-oz.) cans Mexican stewed tomatoes, or Ro*Tel tomatoes

1 cup salsa (mild, medium, or hot, whichever you prefer)

4-oz. can chopped green chilies

14½-oz. can tomato sauce

Tortilla chips

1. Combine all ingredients in large slow cooker.

2. Cover. Cook on Low 8 hours.

3. Just before serving, remove chicken breasts and slice into bite-sized pieces. Stir into soup.

4. Put a handful of tortilla chips in each individual soup bowl. Ladle soup over chips. Top with shredded cheese.

Chicken Tortilla Soup

Becky Fixel, Grosse Pointe Farms, MI

Makes 10–12 servings
Prep. Time: 5 minutes   Cooking Time: 7–8 hours   Ideal slow-cooker size: 5-qt.

2 lb. boneless, skinless chicken breast

32 oz. chicken stock

14 oz. verde sauce

10-oz. can diced tomatoes with lime juice

15-oz. can sweet corn, drained

1 Tbsp. minced garlic

1 small onion, diced

1 Tbsp. chili pepper

½ tsp. fresh ground pepper

½ tsp. salt

½ tsp. oregano

1 Tbsp. dried jalapeño slices

1. Add all ingredients to your slow cooker.

2. Cook on Low for 7–8 hours.

3. Approximately 30 minutes before the end, remove your chicken and shred it into small pieces.

Serving suggestion:

Top with a dollop of non-fat plain Greek yogurt, shredded cheese, fresh jalapeños, or fresh cilantro.

Chicken Chickpea Tortilla Soup

Hope Comerford, Clinton Township, MI

Makes 4–6 servings
Prep. Time: 5 minutes & Cooking Time: 6 hours & Ideal slow-cooker size: 4-qt.

2 boneless, skinless chicken breasts

2 (14½-oz.) cans petite diced tomatoes

15-oz. can garbanzo beans (chickpeas), drained

6 cups gluten–free chicken stock

1 onion, chopped

4-oz. can diced green chilies

1 tsp. cilantro

3–4 fresh garlic cloves, minced

1 tsp. sea salt

1 tsp. pepper

1 tsp. cumin

1 tsp. paprika

1. Place all ingredients in slow cooker.

2. Cover and cook on Low for 6 hours.

3. Use two forks to pull apart chicken into shreds.

Serving suggestion:

Serve with a small dollop of non-fat Greek yogurt, a little shredded cheddar, and some baked blue corn tortilla chips.

Southwest Chicken and White Bean Soup

Karen Ceneviva, Seymour, CT

Makes 6 servings
Prep Time: 15 minutes ⚓ *Cooking Time: 4–10 hours* ⚓ *Ideal slow-cooker size: 3½-qt.*

1 Tbsp. vegetable oil

1 lb. boneless, skinless chicken breasts, cut into 1–inch cubes

1¾ cups chicken broth

1 cup chunky salsa

3 cloves garlic, minced

2 Tbsp. cumin

15½-oz. can small white beans, drained and rinsed

1 cup frozen corn

1 large onion, chopped

1. Heat oil in 10-inch skillet over medium to high heat. Add chicken and cook until it is well browned on all sides. Stir frequently to prevent sticking.

2. Mix broth, salsa, garlic, cumin, beans, corn, and onion in slow cooker. Add chicken. Stir well.

3. Cover. Cook 8–10 hours on Low or 4–5 hours on High.

Black Bean Soup with Chicken and Salsa

Hope Comerford, Clinton Township, MI

Makes 4–6 servings
Prep. Time: 10 minutes ⚜ *Cooking Time: 6–8 hours* ⚜ *Ideal Slow Cooker Size: 5- to 6-qt.*

4 cups chicken broth

I large boneless, skinless chicken breast

2 (15-oz.) cans black beans, drained and rinsed

16-oz. jar salsa

I cup frozen corn

I cup sliced fresh mushrooms

½ red onion, chopped

I jalapeño pepper (whole)

1½ tsp. cumin

Salt and pepper to taste

Optional Toppings:

Shredded cheese

Sour cream

Cilantro

Avocado

1. Place all ingredients except the toppings in slow cooker. Stir.

2. Cover and cook on Low for 6–8 hours.

3. Remove the chicken and shred between two forks. Replace back in the soup and stir.

Variation:

You may chop up the jalapeño for extra heat. Leaving it whole provides the flavor without the heat.

Serving suggestion:

Serve garnished with the optional toppings.

Split Pea with Chicken Soup

Mary E. Wheatley
Mashpee, MA

Makes 6–8 servings
Prep Time: 20 minutes ❧ *Cooking Time: 4–10 hours* ❧ *Ideal slow-cooker size: 5-qt.*

16-oz. pkg. dried split peas

¾ cup finely diced carrots

3 cups cubed raw potatoes

8 cups chicken broth

1 cup diced cooked chicken

1. Combine peas, carrots, potatoes, and chicken broth in slow cooker.

2. Cook on High 4–5 hours, or on Low 8–10 hours, or until all vegetables are tender. Stir after the soup begins to slowly boil.

3. Ten minutes before serving, stir in cooked chicken.

Chicken and Ham Gumbo

Barbara Tenney, Delta, PA

Makes 4 servings
Prep. Time: 20 minutes   ✿   Cooking Time: 6–8 hours   ✿   Ideal slow-cooker size: 4-qt.

1 ½ lb. boneless, skinless chicken thighs

1 Tbsp. oil

10-oz. pkg. frozen okra

½ lb. smoked ham, cut into small chunks

1 ½ cups coarsely chopped onions

1 ½ cups coarsely chopped green peppers

2 or 3 (10-oz.) cans cannellini beans, drained

6 cups chicken broth

2 (10-oz.) cans diced tomatoes with green chilies

2 Tbsp. chopped fresh cilantro

1. Cut chicken into bite-sized pieces. Cook in oil in skillet until no longer pink.

2. Run hot water over okra until pieces separate easily.

3. Combine all ingredients but cilantro in slow cooker.

4. Cover. Cook on Low 6–8 hours. Stir in cilantro before serving.

Variations:

1. Stir in ½ cup long-grain, dry rice with rest of ingredients.

2. Add ¾ tsp. salt and ¼ tsp. pepper with other ingredients.

White Chicken Chili

Lucille Hollinger, Richland, PA

Makes 8 servings
Prep. Time: 10 minutes & Cooking Time: 5–6 hours & Ideal slow-cooker size: 3-qt.

4 cups cubed cooked chicken

2 cups chicken broth

2 (14½-oz.) cans cannellini beans

14½-oz. can garbanzo beans

1 cup shredded white cheddar cheese

¼ cup chopped onion

¼ cup chopped bell pepper

2 tsp. ground cumin

½ tsp. dried oregano

¼ tsp. cayenne pepper

¼ tsp. salt

1. Combine all ingredients in slow cooker.

2. Cover and cook on Low for 5–6 hours.

Variations:

Omit garbanzo beans. Shred chicken instead of cubing it. Add 1 tsp. Italian herb seasoning.

—Beverly Hummel

TIP
Best served with sour cream, shredded cheese and tortilla chips, with cornbread on the side.

White Bean and Chicken Chili

Hope Comerford, Clinton Township, MI

Makes 6–8 servings

Prep. Time: 15 minutes ♣ *Cooking Time: 8–10 hours* ♣ *Ideal slow-cooker size: 5-qt.*

2 lb. boneless, skinless chicken, cut into bite-sized chunks

½ cup dry navy beans, soaked overnight, drained, and rinsed

½ cup dry great northern beans, soaked overnight, drained, and rinsed

½ cup chopped carrots

1½ cups chopped onion

14½-oz. can petite diced tomatoes

10-oz. can diced tomatoes with lime juice and cilantro

5 cloves garlic, minced

6-oz. can tomato paste

1 Tbsp. cumin

1 Tbsp. chili powder

1 tsp. salt

¼ tsp. pepper

8 tsp. Better than Bouillon chicken base

8 cups water

1. Place all ingredients into the crock and stir to mix well.

2. Cover and cook on Low for 8–10 hours.

Chicken Barley Chili

Colleen Heatwole, Burton, MI

Makes 10 servings
Prep. Time: 20 minutes ❧ *Cooking Time: 6–8 hours* ❧ *Ideal slow-cooker size: 6-qt.*

2 (14½-oz.) cans diced tomatoes

16-oz. jar salsa

1 cup quick-cooking barley, uncooked

3 cups water

1¾ cups chicken stock

15½-oz. can black beans,
rinsed and drained

3 cups cubed cooked chicken or turkey

15¼-oz. can whole-kernel
corn, undrained

1–3 tsp. chili powder, depending
on how hot you like your chili

1 tsp. cumin

1 tsp. salt

⅛ tsp. pepper

1. Combine all ingredients in slow cooker.

2. Cover. Cook on Low 6–8 hours, or until barley is tender.

Serving suggestion:

Serve in individual soup bowls topped with sour cream and shredded cheese.

Chili Chicken Stew with Rice

Jenny R. Unternahrer, Wayland, IA

Makes 4–5 servings

Prep. Time: 30 minutes   ⚶   Cooking Time: 2½–5 hours   ⚶   Ideal slow-cooker size: 2½-qt.

1½ lb. chicken tenders*

½ small onion, diced

15-oz. can black beans, drained (not rinsed)

14½-oz. can petite diced tomatoes, undrained

1 cup whole corn, drained if needed (thawed if frozen)

2 tsp. chili powder

½ tsp. cumin

2–4 dashes cayenne pepper

1½ tsp. salt

2 cups cooked brown rice

Sour cream, to taste

Shredded Mexican blend cheese, to taste

*You can try whole boneless, skinless chicken breast, but allow more time to cook.

1. Add all the ingredients, except brown rice, sour cream, and shredded cheese, to crock.

2. Mix. Cover and cook on High for 2½ hours or Low for 5 hours.

3. Shred chicken; stir to incorporate.

4. Serve over brown rice and add desired amount of sour cream and shredded Mexican blend cheese.

Metric Equivalent Measurements

If you're accustomed to using metric measurements, I don't want you to be inconvenienced by the imperial measurements I use in this book.

Use this handy chart, too, to figure out the size of the slow cooker you'll need for each recipe.

Weight (Dry Ingredients)

1 oz		30 g
4 oz	¼ lb	120 g
8 oz	½ lb	240 g
12 oz	¾ lb	360 g
16 oz	1 lb	480 g
32 oz	2 lb	960 g

Slow Cooker Sizes

1-quart	0.96 l
2-quart	1.92 l
3-quart	2.88 l
4-quart	3.84 l
5-quart	4.80 l
6-quart	5.76 l
7-quart	6.72 l
8-quart	7.68 l

Volume (Liquid Ingredients)

½ tsp.		2 ml
1 tsp.		5 ml
1 Tbsp.	½ fl oz	15 ml
2 Tbsp.	1 fl oz	30 ml
¼ cup	2 fl oz	60 ml
⅓ cup	3 fl oz	80 ml
½ cup	4 fl oz	120 ml
⅔ cup	5 fl oz	160 ml
¾ cup	6 fl oz	180 ml
1 cup	8 fl oz	240 ml
1 pt	16 fl oz	480 ml
1 qt	32 fl oz	960 ml

Length

¼ in	6 mm
½ in	13 mm
¾ in	19 mm
1 in	25 mm
6 in	15 cm
12 in	30 cm

Recipe and Ingredient Index

Chicken and Corn Soup, 297
Chicken and Vegetables, 111
Chicken Casablanca, 189
Chicken Curry, 197
Chicken in a Pot, 99
Chicken Sweet and Sour, 151
Chicken with Vegetables in Gravy, 113
Curried Chicken Dinner, 85
Greek Chicken, 107
Honey Balsamic Chicken, 181
Lemon Pepper Chicken and Veggies, 41
Orange Chicken and Sweet Potatoes, 175
Split Pea with Chicken Soup, 309
Sweet Potato Chicken Casserole, 227
Uncle Tim's Chicken and Sauerkraut, 81

Q

Quickie Barbecued Chicken, 83

R

Rachel's Chicken Casserole, 217
raisins
    Chicken Casablanca, 189
    Chicken Curry, 197
    Chicken Mole, 183
ranch dressing mix
    Salsa Ranch Chicken with Black Beans, 143
Raspberried Chicken Drumsticks, 35
red peppers
    Barbara's Creole Chicken, 199
    Healthy Chicken Chow Mein, 203
    Orange Chicken Leg Quarters, 177
    Slow-Cooker Chicken Fajitas, 139
    Slow-Cooker Tex-Mex Chicken, 137
    Sweet 'N' Sour Chicken with Veggies, 89
relish
    Heavenly Barbecued Chicken Wings, 253
    Tracy's Barbecued Chicken Wings, 261
rice
    brown
        Chicken Mole, 183
        Chicken Vegetable Dish, 167
        Chili Chicken Stew with Rice, 319
        Slow-Cooker Chicken and Salsa, 141
        Wild Rice-Chicken-Sausage Bake, 221
    Chicken and Vegetable Soup with Rice, 291
    Chicken Curry with Rice, 87
    Chicken Rice Soup, 287
    Chicken with Broccoli Rice, 225
    Jambalaya, 201
    Mary's Chicken and Rice Soup, 289
    Simple Chicken Rice Soup, 285
    wild
        Chicken Rice Soup, 287

Wild Rice-Chicken-Sausage Bake, 221
Roast Chicken, 17
Rosemarie's Barbecued Chicken Wings, 259
rosemary
    Honey Balsamic Chicken, 181
Russian dressing
    Chicken à la Orange, 57
    Chicken in Piquant Sauce, 51
    Rachel's Chicken Casserole, 217

S

sage
    Stuffed Chicken Rolls, 193
salsa
    Easy Chicken Tortilla Soup, 299
    Slow-Cooker Chicken and Salsa, 141
    Slow-Cooker Tex-Mex Chicken, 137
    Southwest Chicken and White Bean Soup, 305
    Thai Chicken, 45
Salsa Ranch Chicken with Black Beans, 143
sauerkraut
    Chicken Reuben Bake, 223
    Rachel's Chicken Casserole, 217
    Uncle Tim's Chicken and Sauerkraut, 81
sausage
    Andouille
        Jambalaya, 201
    Italian
        Wild Rice-Chicken-Sausage Bake, 221
Savory Slow-Cooker Chicken, 163
shallots
    Barbara's Creole Chicken, 199
    Garlic and Lemon Chicken, 123
shrimp
    Jambalaya, 201
Simple Chicken, 65
Simple Chicken Rice Soup, 285
Slow-Cooker Chicken and Dumplings, 159
Slow-Cooker Chicken and Salsa, 141
Slow-Cooker Chicken Fajitas, 139
Slow-Cooker Tex-Mex Chicken, 137
snow peas
    Teriyaki Chicken, 91
soda crackers
    Elizabeth's Hot Chicken Sandwiches, 243
sour cream
    Black Bean Soup with Chicken and Salsa, 307
    Chicken Made Easy, 67
    Chicken with Vegetables in Gravy, 113
    Slow-Cooker Chicken and Salsa, 141
Southwest Chicken and White Bean Soup, 305
soy sauce
    California Chicken, 101
    Chicken Chow Mein, 61

About the Author

Hope Comerford is a mom, wife, elementary music teacher, blogger, recipe developer, public speaker, ALM Zone Fitness Motivator, Young Living Essential Oils essential oil enthusiast/educator and published author. In 2013, she was diagnosed with a severe gluten intolerance and since then has spent many hours creating easy, practical and delicious gluten–free recipes that can be enjoyed by both those who are affected by gluten and those who are not.

Growing up, Hope spent many hours in the kitchen with her Meme (grandmother) and her love for cooking grew from there. While working on her master's degree when her daughter was young, Hope turned to her slow cookers for some salvation and sanity. It was from there she began truly experimenting with recipes and quickly learned she had the ability to get a little more creative in the kitchen and develop her own recipes.

In 2010, Hope started her blog, *A Busy Mom's Slow Cooker Adventures* to simply share the recipes she was making with her family and friends. She never imagined people all over the world would begin visiting her page and sharing her recipes with others as well. In 2013, Hope self–published her first cookbook *Slow Cooker Recipes 10 Ingredients or Less and Gluten–Free* and then later wrote *The Gluten–Free Slow Cooker*.

Hope is thrilled to be working with Fix–It and Forget–It and to be representing such an iconic line of cookbooks. She is excited to bring her creativeness to the Fix–It and Forget–It brand. Through Fix–It and Forget–It, Hope has written many books, including *Fix–It and Forget–It Lazy & Slow, Fix–It and Forget–It Healthy Slow Cooker Cookbook, Fix–It and Forget–It Favorite Slow Cooker Recipes for Mom, Fix–It and Forget–It Favorite Slow Cooker Recipes for Dad, and Fix–It and Forget–It Instant Pot Cookbook*. Hope lives in the city of Clinton Township, Michigan, near Metro Detroit and is a Michigan native. She has been happily married to her husband and best friend Justin since 2008. Together they have 2 children, Ella and Gavin, who are her motivation, inspiration, and heart. In her spare time, Hope enjoys traveling, singing, cooking, reading books, spending time with friends and family, and relaxing.